IN THE KITCHEN WITH BOB

Christmas Collection

IN THE KITCHEN WITH BOB

Christmas

Collection

QVC PUBLISHING, INC.

QVC Publishing, Inc.
Jill Cohen, Vice President and Publisher
Ellen Bruzelius, General Manager
Sarah Butterworth, Editorial Director
Cassandra Reynolds, Publishing Assistant

Produced in association with Patrick Filley Associates, Inc.
Design by Joel Avirom and Jason Snyder
Photography by Mark Thomas Studio
Prop styling by Nancy Micklin
Food Styling by Ann Disrude

 Publishing and colophon are trademarks of QVC Publishing, Inc.

Published by QVC Publishing, Inc., 50 Main Street, Mt. Kisco, New York 10549

Manufactured in Hong Kong

ISBN: 1-928998-03-8

First Edition

10 9 8 7 6 5 4 3 2 1

Contents

Introduction

My earliest memories of Christmas are of people. To be sure, there are the warm, faded images of Christmas trees past, red and white furred stockings lining the fronts of fireplaces, candles flickering in windows, holly and pinecones scenting every cubic inch of the house, stacks of presents waiting to be opened and a big, golden turkey—there was always a huge turkey with all the trimmings in the dining room. But what I remember most are crowds of people around the house throughout the holidays: visitors, carolers, family and extended family, pastors, choir members, neighbors, folks from Dad's work and a gazillion kids—cousins, second cousins, infants, toddlers, teens and "the older kids" (they always hung out by themselves). I was always in the middle of a crowd, and I loved it.

You see, my parents believed that Christmas was a group thing, that time of year when you put aside most everything else and came together with those closest and most important to you. You rekindled friendships that circumstances made distant, you caught up with all the changes, you celebrated each other's having made it through another year. You exchanged gifts both major and minor. You opened your home to family and friends. There were parties, open houses, caroling nights, brunches and breakfasts and dinners.

And at the heart of it all was the food. Every table was filled—kitchen, dining room, living room, coffee table, hallway sideboards—whether it was the afternoon we set up and decorated the tree, or the frigid night that the church choir came over and we all went out caroling and came back for Dad's cider or creamy hot chocolate. The house was permeated with the sweet and savory air of the holidays—roasting turkeys, sweet potatoes stuffed with the unmistakable scent of butter, brown sugar and marshmallows, pies whose sweet, fruity scents seduced you from the next room, spicy cookies beckoning from the cooling racks, the rich, dark fragrance of homemade fudge stacked on the counter—it was a cornucopia of holiday delights that will forever remain in my sensory memory.

I suppose it would have been simpler for me to have just collected all those wonderful recipes and categorized them for you here, but that didn't strike me as the most appropriate way for me to bring you the best I have for Christmas. Because, as I said above, the Christmas season for me was one of many celebrations, many gatherings, all special in their own way, each with its own distinct features and flavors.

So, the more I mulled it over, the closer I came to the conclusion that what I really must do—for you, as well as in honor of my parents and their love of the holidays—was to put together some of the "blueprints" of the types of gatherings we enjoyed. After all, one of the main reasons we tend not to do these kinds of things is that there's so much planning that has to be done in advance, right at the time of year when time for planning is practically nonexistent.

I mean, who has time to coordinate the menu for an open house for 24 when you still have 20 presents to buy and wrap, three dozen Christmas cards to sign and mail, and at least two school Christmas pageants to attend?

So let me make some suggestions. I've put this book together in sections, so you can pick and choose from any number of celebratory gatherings. There are menus for an Open House, a Tree-Trimming Party, Caroling parties, Christmas Eve Dinner, and Christmas Day breakfast. And I've included three different Christmas dinners, one of which, the Elegant Holiday Dinner, was the one Mom always made for us. That was her baby, and she captained it from start to finish, marshaling each of us in the family, assigning us different duties, which we gladly took on knowing the glory and pleasure the end result would afford us.

And in the spirit of the season, I offer a selection of Gifts from the Kitchen, confections and concoctions that carry a little of yourself with them as you give them to family and friends. Nothing here is difficult, but just the sound of their names—Christmas Crescents, Scottish Shortbread, Gateau Bourbon Spice Cake, Brandied Apricot Jam, Pear Chutney, Butterscotch Sauce, Tangerine-Fig Relish, Almond Brittle, Bourbon Balls and a dozen different jams, jellies and cookies—will make whoever you give them to feel special, and know that you took a little extra time for them this year. One hint here: you might want to make a double batch—one for them, one for you. There should be a "To Me, From Me" present under the tree every year.

As you make your plans for the holidays, I hope you'll find something in this book to make that special time a little simpler, a little more enjoyable, a little richer. Of course, feel free to mix and match any recipe from any menu, or just select one or two to try anytime. They're my gifts to you, to enjoy whenever you wish. May you have the warmest of holidays, and the best of the new year.

MENUS
FOR THE
CHRISTMAS SEASON

Tree Trimming Supper for 16

Caroling Celebration for 20

Holiday Open House for 16 to 20

Italian Christmas Eve Dinner for 8

Christmas Breakfast for 4 to 6

Holiday Brunch for 16

Christmas Feast for 8

Country Christmas Supper for 12

Elegant Holiday Dinner for 12

$\mathcal{E}$ach of these menus has its own special recipes. The Open House has light, easy ideas that take little time, and, since there's no specific moment that all the food has to hit the table, a lot of it can be done in advance. I remember Dad starting a few days ahead of our annual open house—baking the cookies (and hiding them from us kids, who would have eaten every last one of them had we found them), making some eggnog, putting the skewers together and letting them sit in a marinade in the fridge, setting up the various rooms with plates and utensils. This way he and Mom weren't rushed the day of the party. The dishes were always kept simple too, so any work done that day could be done quickly and without elaborate preparation. A quick glaze for a ham or a turkey, and the oven does the rest. A few ingredients in a blender for a salad dressing, some quick combining of lettuces, and you have the salad. And since most of the guests at an open house are wandering, whatever is served should be light, easily served and portable.

The Tree Trimming Supper is a nice mixture of finger foods and a sit-down dinner. Things like Artichoke Puffs and Apricots Wrapped in Bacon are great to pop in your mouth as you hang the next ball or star on the bough, and the Mulled Wine will keep spirits warm and festive. Once the tree is lit and radiant—only Mom was allowed to declare the tree complete by placing the angel ornament on the top—a Roasted Rack of Lamb can be waiting and ready, surrounded by a Squash and Carrot Puree, and Snow Peas Sautéed with Shallots.

The Caroling Celebration, like the Open House, is made for larger crowds who will "graze," as my dad put it—wander from table to table, stop and chat, grab a bite or two and then move on to the next area of interest. Again, a lot of it can be made in advance of the caroling evening. And since it's probably going to be pretty nippy outside, the menu choices will all have a little "heat" to them: a spicy Shrimp Bisque, Buffalo Wings with a toasty Red Chili Sauce, a warm Vegetarian Chili, and, of course, a Mulled Cider upon your return (Dad always supplemented this with a rich hot chocolate as well).

The Italian Christmas Eve Dinner included here represents an homage to my wife Toni's side of the family. Her Italian heritage offers a special way to celebrate the night before Christmas, with classics like Stracciatella (another great recipe from the kitchens of her many aunts), a marvelous Pan-Roasted Salmon, and classic Tuscan side dishes like Fagioli alla Toscana and Broccoli Rabe. And is there anything better at Christmas than chocolate? Wait till you taste the Chocolate Semifreddo!

Christmas Breakfast for the Bowersoxes was one of the most exciting meals of the year—not so much for the great Sour Cream Pancakes or Omelets that Dad would make us, or the baked goods he'd pull out of his secret hiding place (the same place he stashed the cookies), but because we weren't allowed to catch even a glimpse of our presents or stockings until breakfast was enjoyed by one and all! It was exquisite agony—savoring the pancakes or the fruity muffins, while all the while trying to sit still in the chairs, anticipating the fun and joy of what would inevitably follow. But there's something wonderful about not wolfing down a quick bowl of cereal on that most special of mornings...something special about taking the time with family to cook and eat a pleasant meal together before moving into the day.

But if you'd like something more elaborate for Christmas Day, I've included some suggestions for a larger Holiday Brunch—ideas that have a more elegant feel while still being easy to accomplish on a busy morning. I particularly like this idea for those who would enjoy opening their doors on Christmas morning, or having some folks back after church. There's such a wonderful mix of scents and flavors—Almond French Toast, a Sausage and Potato Frittata, Pumpkin Scones—a sensory brightness that will match the joy of a Christmas morning.

And then there's Christmas dinner. If there's one meal with my family that I will always hold dear, it's this one. I can taste the roast turkey, and the cornbread stuffing, the sweet potatoes and the chocolate cake. If I could choose one moment in my life to revisit, it would be one of those Christmas dinners.

I've included three different Christmas dinners for you—a Christmas Feast that features a continental touch with Prosciutto and Wilted Greens, Beef Tenderloin with Port-Rosemary Sauce, Pommes à la Dauphinoise and Christmas Pudding with Hard Sauce. Then there's the simpler Country Christmas Supper, with Butternut Squash Soup, Buttermilk Biscuits, Pork Medallions with Mandarin Oranges and Cranberries, Roasted Root Vegetables, and my father's famous Serious Pecan Pie. And lastly, there's the Elegant Holiday Dinner—my mother's masterpiece—with a Lobster Bisque, Rosemary Roasted Turkey, Corn Bread Stuffing with Cranberries and Pecans, Sweet Potato Batons and a rich Flourless Chocolate Cake.

I can still feel the warmth in the dining room, see the glow of a dozen candles on the table covered in white linen and lace, hear the sound of a dozen people laughing and teasing, and the clink of silverware and wine goblets as we partook of the bounty God had granted us.

Tree Trimming Supper for 16

Mulled Wine

Roasted Peppers and
Artichoke Puffs

Dried Apricots
Wrapped in Bacon

Roasted Rack of Lamb
with Pecan and
Cilantro Crust

Butternut Squash
and Carrot Puree

Snow Peas Sautéed
with Shallots

Chocolate-Dipped Fruit

Mulled Wine

A FAVORITE WINTER DRINK IN EUROPE since medieval times, particularly in the mountainous regions of Germany and Scandinavia, hot spiced wine is enjoyable before or after a meal. It is traditionally prepared by slowly heating the contents of a bottle of Bordeaux or Burgundy with spices. Adjust the amount of sugar used to suit your individual taste.

1	cup sugar
½	cup water
20	whole cloves
1	cinnamon stick
½	teaspoon freshly grated nutmeg or ground
1	2-inch piece gingerroot
	Peel of 1 orange
	Peel of 1 lemon
3	quarts dry red wine
	Lemon, thinly sliced, for garnish

In a small saucepot, boil the first 8 ingredients for 5 minutes until they make a syrup. Place the wine in a 4-quart pot. Strain the syrup into the wine. Just before serving, bring the mixture to a boil and ladle into mugs. Garnish with a thin slice of lemon.

Roasted Peppers and Artichoke Puffs

MAKES 24

FESTIVE RED, YELLOW AND ORANGE bell peppers make this hors d'oeuvre a colorful addition to the table. Topped with a savory mixture of chopped artichokes, crumbled bacon, grated Swiss cheese and seasonings, these are bound to be a hit. To accommodate the busy cook, they can be prepared hours in advance and quickly broiled just before serving.

½   bunch green onions, minced

1   garlic clove, minced

1   tablespoon unsalted butter

1   6-ounce can artichoke bottoms, drained, diced

2   slices bacon, cooked, drained, crumbled

2   tablespoons chopped fresh parsley

¼   cup grated Swiss cheese

2   teaspoons lemon juice

    Freshly ground pepper to taste

¼   cup mayonnaise

2   red bell peppers

2   orange bell peppers

2   yellow bell peppers

2   tablespoons olive oil

1   tablespoon balsamic vinegar

    Salt and freshly ground pepper to taste

In a small sauté pan over medium heat, cook the green onions and garlic in the butter until soft. Place in a mixing bowl and add the artichokes, bacon, parsley and Swiss cheese. Sprinkle with the lemon juice and pepper and toss well. Mix in the mayonnaise, cover and chill for at least an hour.

Preheat the oven to 400°F. Cut off the tops and bottoms of the peppers. Make 1 cut down the side of each and remove the seeds and white inner fibers. Cut the peppers into large triangles. You should have 4 triangles per pepper. Place the peppers in a shallow baking pan, drizzle with the olive oil and vinegar and sprinkle with the salt and pepper. Roast for 15 minutes, stirring once while they are cooking. Remove from the oven and cool.

Just before serving, turn the oven on to broil. Place 1 full tablespoon of the artichoke mixture onto each triangle and broil on a baking sheet until bubbly. Cool slightly and serve.

Dried Apricots Wrapped in Bacon

MAKES 24

THE SURPRISE PAIRING OF sweet apricots and savory bacon slices in this hors d'oeuvre makes it a hands-down favorite at every party. Always the first to disappear, it's a snap to prepare in advance. Just be sure to let the pieces cool a bit before serving because they are very hot when taken directly from the oven.

8   slices bacon (about ½ pound)

24   dried apricots

Toothpicks (soaked in water for at least 15 minutes)

Preheat the broiler. Cut each slice of bacon into 3 pieces. Wrap each apricot with a piece of bacon and secure with a toothpick. On a baking sheet, broil the apricots 4 inches from the flame for about 5 minutes or until the bacon is brown. Remove the pan from the oven and turn over each apricot. Return the pan to the oven and broil for an additional 5 to 10 minutes, until brown.

Remove the apricots from the pan onto a paper towel to drain. Allow to cool slightly.

Roasted Rack of Lamb with Pecan and Cilantro Crust

SERVES 16

RACK OF LAMB IS ELEGANT and relatively easy to prepare. Ask the butcher to "french" the rack, which is scraping the bones clean from the meat portion to the end. This improves the lamb's presentation and prevents excess fat from collecting on the plate.

2 cups pecans, toasted

12 garlic cloves, peeled

4 cups fresh cilantro leaves

1 cup fresh lemon juice

2 cups freshly grated Parmesan cheese

1 cup olive oil

Salt and freshly ground pepper to taste

8 racks of lamb, trimmed

Toast the pecans in a preheated 350°F oven until brown, about 5 to 7 minutes. Let cool. In the bowl of a food processor, place the garlic and pecans. Pulse until it becomes a paste. Add the cilantro, lemon juice, Parmesan and olive oil and process until smooth. Season with the salt and pepper.

Preheat the oven to 450°F. Cover the exposed lamb bones with foil to avoid their becoming charred. Place the lamb on a rack in a large roasting pan. Press the paste onto the meat and roast for 20 minutes. Remove from the oven and allow the meat to rest for 10 minutes before carving. Using a long knife, carve the lamb by cutting between the bones. Allow 2 to 3 chops per serving.

Butternut Squash and Carrot Puree

MOVE OVER MASHED POTATOES! The sweet, buttery smoothness of this vivid orange vegetable dish makes it a hit with all ages and a perfect accompaniment to roasted rack of lamb. It has the added bonus of being fast to assemble and can be prepared in advance, then reheated in the oven or microwave just before serving.

9 pounds butternut squash (about 4), peeled, cut into 2-inch cubes

2 pounds carrots (about 10), peeled, cut into 2-inch pieces

½ pound unsalted butter, room temperature

¼ cup brown sugar

Salt and freshly ground pepper to taste

Place the squash and carrots in 2 medium pots and cover with cold water. Bring to a boil. Cook for 10 minutes, until fork tender.

In the bowl of a food processor, put equal amounts of squash, carrots, butter and sugar. Puree until smooth. Repeat until all of the carrots and squash are pureed. Season with salt and pepper to taste.

Snow Peas Sautéed with Shallots

SERVES 16

BRILLIANT GREEN SNOW PEAS are an eye-catching side dish at any winter dinner. While it takes a bit of time to pinch off the ends and destring the snow peas, this can be done a day or two before cooking. Then sautéing this colorful vegetable takes only a matter of minutes. Be sure to serve them immediately to maximize their sweet flavor and crunchiness.

8   tablespoons (1 stick) unsalted butter

4   medium shallots, minced

3   pounds snow peas, tops and strings removed

    Salt to taste

In a large sauté pan over medium heat, melt the butter. Turn up the heat to high and add the shallots and half of the snow peas. Sauté, shaking the pan or turning the snow-peas with a metal spatula until they begin to soften. Remove from the heat and quickly add the rest of the snow peas. Cook in the same manner. Toss the 2 batches of snow peas together, sprinkle with the salt and serve immediately.

Chocolate-Dipped Fruit

MAKES 30 PIECES

THIS DISH CAN BE PREPARED A DAY in advance and kept uncovered in the refrigerator. Do not cover with plastic wrap—this will create condensation on the chocolate and make the fruit soggy.

16 tablespoons (2 sticks) unsalted butter

12 ounces high-quality semisweet chocolate

20 pieces mixed fruits (such as strawberries, apples, oranges, tangerines, pears and peaches), cut into sections

½ cup finely chopped pistachio nuts (optional)

In the top of a double boiler, melt the butter and chocolate over simmering water. Stir just to blend thoroughly. Remove the chocolate from the double boiler and keep warm, about body temperature.

Section or cut the pieces of fruit. Cover a large tray with waxed paper. Dip each piece of fruit halfway into the chocolate. Hold the fruit over the chocolate to allow excess chocolate to drain off. Place the dipped fruit on the waxed paper, sprinkle with the pistachios (if desired) and refrigerate until the chocolate is set. Just before serving, gently peel the fruit from the waxed paper and place on a decorative plate.

CAROLING

CELEBRATION FOR 20

Mulled Cider

Shrimp Bisque

Roasted Onion-Tomato
   Crostini

Buffalo Wings with
   Red Chili Sauce

Vegetarian Chili

Rice Pilaf

Spinach Salad

Corn Bread Sticks

Ginger Apple Upside-Down
   Cake

Mulled Cider

On a wintry afternoon, few things are more inviting than the aroma of hot spiced apple cider wafting through the house, or holding a warm mug against chilled fingers. Dark brown sugar gives this version its rich sweetness, while clove-studded apple "stars" add a festive touch to the serving bowl. Stir in a jigger of brandy or rum to boost the warming effect.

1½	gallons apple cider
1	pound dark brown sugar
6	cinnamon sticks
½	teaspoon freshly grated nutmeg or ground
2	large apples
20	whole cloves

In a large, nonreactive saucepot, heat the cider, brown sugar, cinnamon and nutmeg. Simmer for 15 minutes.

While the cider is heating, cut the apples crosswise into ½-inch-thick slices. With a star-shaped cookie cutter that fits the size of the slice, punch out stars. Stud the stars with the cloves.

When the cider is heated, pour it into a decorative bowl and float the apple stars in it.

Shrimp Bisque

SERVES 20

THE COOKING TERM "BISQUE" WAS USED for centuries to label creamy meat or game soups. In the 17th century, crayfish – and hence other shellfish – became the primary ingredient. Thrifty cooks will appreciate the traditional method of using the entire shrimp in this soup: shells to season the stock and shrimp meat for texture. For the best flavor, look for shrimp that has never been frozen.

 5 pounds medium shrimp

10 cups chicken stock

 1 bay leaf

¾ cup (1½ sticks) unsalted butter

½ cup chopped celery

 1 cup chopped onions

 1 cup chopped carrots

¼ teaspoon marjoram

¼ teaspoon freshly grated nutmeg or ground

 5 cups heavy cream

    Salt and white pepper to taste

Peel and devein the shrimp, adding the shells to the chicken stock. Cut the shrimp into ½-inch pieces and set aside. Heat the stock with the bay leaf and shells and bring to a boil. Immediately lower the heat and let simmer gently for 20 minutes. Strain the stock into a large pot.

In a large sauté pan, melt the butter. Add the celery, onions and carrots and cook over a low heat until the onions become clear. Add the spices and cook for an additional minute. In a food processor, puree the vegetable mix. Gradually add 3 cups of the cream.

Reheat the stock. Add the vegetable and cream mixture and the shrimp. Simmer until the shrimp are opaque. Adjust the consistency of the bisque with the remaining 2 cups of cream. Add the salt and white pepper to taste.

Roasted Onion-Tomato Crostini

MAKES ABOUT 32 PIECES

CRISP FRENCH BREAD SLICES TOPPED with a warm puree of tomatoes and red onion are an easy appetizer to serve at a holiday gathering of family and friends. Simply roast the vegetables in advance, then prepare and refrigerate the pureed mixture up to two days before assembling these colorful toast slices.

Cooking spray or olive oil

2 **large red onions, cut into ½-inch-thick slices**

¼ **cup red wine vinegar**

3 **pounds plum tomatoes, cut into ¼-inch-thick slices**

Salt and freshly ground pepper to taste

32 **½-inch-thick slices crusty Italian or French bread**

Preheat the oven to 450°F.

Spray 3 baking pans with cooking spray or wipe with olive oil. Arrange the onion slices in a single layer in 2 of the pans and drizzle the vinegar over them. Overlap the tomatoes on the onions and bake until the tomatoes are browned on the edges, about 30 minutes.

Transfer the vegetables to a food processor or blender and process until coarsely pureed. Season to taste with salt and pepper.

Place the bread slices on the remaining baking sheet and broil about 5 inches below the heat. Turn once, until just golden on each side. Spread each piece with the pureed vegetables, then flash broil again until the onion-tomato mixture is just warm. Serve immediately.

Buffalo Wings with Red Chili Sauce

MAKES 35 WINGS

FINGER-LICKING GOOD, THESE SPICY hors d'oeuvres always please a party crowd. Just remember, the longer the chicken wings marinate, the spicier they will become, so judge the amount of marinade time against your guests' taste buds. Serve these crisp, zesty wings with homemade red chili sauce for extra punch.

BUFFALO WINGS

- 2 cups red wine vinegar
- 2 tablespoons chili powder
- 2 teaspoons salt
- 2 teaspoons freshly ground pepper
- 2 teaspoons vegetable oil
- 2 teaspoons Worcestershire sauce
- ¼ cup hot pepper sauce (such as Tabasco)
- 35 chicken wings

RED CHILI SAUCE

- 1 cup sour cream
- ¼ cup mayonnaise
- 2 tablespoons chili powder
- 1 teaspoon ground cumin

FOR BUFFALO WINGS: In a small bowl, combine the vinegar, chili powder, salt, pepper, oil, Worcestershire sauce and hot pepper sauce. Rinse the wings and pat them dry. Put the wings and marinade in 2 large food storage bags and shake to coat the wings. Let stand for at least 30 minutes and up to 12 hours. Preheat the grill or broiler to high. Cook the wings, basting throughout and turning, until they are golden brown and crisp—about 15 minutes.

FOR RED CHILI SAUCE: Combine all of the ingredients for the sauce and store up to 5 days in the refrigerator. Serve at room temperature alongside the wings or in a separate dipping bowl.

Vegetarian Chili

CHILI IS VERSATILE, HEALTHY AND HEARTY. Don't be afraid to include different types of beans besides the ones called for here—black, chickpeas, etc.—and even corn or peas to this recipe. They will all bring flavor, color and protein. Prepare this a day or two before serving, or freeze for a couple of weeks to allow the flavors to meld.

8   large onions, chopped

⅓   cup corn oil

2   large green bell peppers, seeded, chopped

2   tablespoons mustard seeds

2   tablespoons chili powder

2   teaspoons cumin seeds

2   teaspoons unsweetened cocoa

½   teaspoon ground cinnamon

12   ounces tomato paste

32   ounces canned tomatoes

64   ounces canned kidney beans, undrained

2   cups water

Salt and freshly ground pepper to taste

Lime wedges

In a large, heavy pot over medium-high heat, cook the onions in the corn oil until they become translucent. Add the green peppers and mustard seeds and stir for 1 minute. Add the chili powder, cumin seeds, cocoa, cinnamon and tomato paste and cook for another minute. Add the tomatoes and kidney beans in their liquid, reduce the heat and simmer, uncovered, for about 40 minutes. Add the water and stir as needed to prevent the chili from scorching.

Season with salt and pepper to taste. Serve with the lime wedges.

Corn Bread Sticks

THIS CORN BREAD IS PARTICULARLY flavorful because of the use of corn kernels. It is not necessary to use fresh corn, which is difficult to find in the winter, so use either frozen or drained, canned kernels. These corn bread sticks can also be baked ahead and frozen for a few days. Reheat just before serving.

3 cups all-purpose flour

1½ cups yellow cornmeal

¼ cup sugar

4 teaspoons baking powder

1 teaspoon baking soda

1 teaspoon salt

2 cups corn kernels

¼ cup chopped onion

4 eggs

2½ cups buttermilk

½ cup unsalted butter, melted

Corn oil

Preheat the oven to 350°F. Place corn stick molds into the oven for 5 minutes or until ready to use.

In a large mixing bowl, place the dry ingredients, the corn and onion. Stir until combined. In another bowl, whisk together the eggs, buttermilk and butter. Add the buttermilk mixture to the cornmeal mixture and stir until just combined.

Brush the molds with the oil and spoon the batter into the molds until they are ½ filled. Bake for 15 to 20 minutes, until the sticks are golden brown. Allow to cool for 2 minutes and then turn them out onto a rack to cool slightly. Repeat the process, brushing the mold with oil before each batch, until the batter is gone.

Serve warm, placed in a basket lined with a linen napkin.

Ginger Apple Upside-Down Cake

SERVES 20

UPSIDE-DOWN CAKES—WHERE THE BOTTOM of the cake turns into its top—are another of those delightful "comfort foods" that bring back happy childhood memories for many of us. This version with apples and spices is a different twist on traditional gingerbread. A scoop of vanilla or cinnamon ice cream, or a dollop of whipped cream on the side extends the bliss.

½	cup unsalted butter
½	cup light brown sugar
¼	cup light corn syrup
5	to 6 firm apples, cored, cut into ¼-inch wedges
4	cups all-purpose flour
1	cup sugar
4	teaspoons baking powder
1	teaspoon salt
½	teaspoon baking soda
1½	teaspoons ground ginger
2	teaspoons ground cinnamon
½	teaspoon allspice
¼	teaspoon ground cloves
12	tablespoons (1½ sticks) unsalted butter, melted
2	cups water
1⅓	cups unsulphured molasses
2	teaspoons freshly grated gingerroot
	Whipped cream

Preheat the oven to 350°F. In a small, nonstick pot, heat the ½ cup butter, brown sugar and corn syrup until melted. Stir to combine.

In 2 9-inch round cake pans, arrange the apple slices in a circular fashion, letting the apples slightly overlap. Pour the brown sugar syrup over the apples.

Sift together the dry ingredients. Add the 12 tablespoons butter, the water, molasses and gingerroot. Mix well and pour over the apples. Gently tap the pans against the counter to settle the batter.

Bake the cakes for 45 to 50 minutes, until they begin to pull from the sides and a toothpick inserted into the center comes out clean. Allow them to rest for 10 minutes. Flip onto a serving plate and readjust the apples into a tidy arrangement. Serve warm with whipped cream.

Holiday Open House

FOR 16 TO 20

Eggnog

Spiced Fruit
Sparkle Punch

Banderillas

Shrimp Puffs

Mustard and
Fruit Glazed Ham

Raspberry Glazed Turkey

Rice with Caramelized
Onion, Brandy
and Red Bell Pepper

Baby Carrots with Mustard
and Parsley

Romaine and Red Leaf
Lettuce Salad

Bûche de Nöel

Eggnog

Eggnog is traditionally made with raw eggs, which we all now avoid for health reasons. Using store-bought eggnog may feel like cheating, but it makes fast work of a party punch and the worry about bacteria is minimized.

4 quarts prepared eggnog

½ teaspoon freshly grated nutmeg or ground

2 fifths (51.2 ounces) light rum

1 quart vanilla ice cream

A half hour before serving, mix the eggnog, half the nutmeg and the rum in a large punch bowl. Cut the ice cream into large chunks and float them in the punch. Just before serving, stir the mixture and sprinkle with the remaining nutmeg.

Spiced Fruit Sparkle Punch

Makes 30 servings

Use the best local apple cider you can find for the freshest flavor for this fruity punch. Increase or lessen the amount of seltzer you use to achieve the degree of sweetness you want.

3 gallons apple cider

2 gallons cranberry juice cocktail

2 2-liter bottles seltzer

2 2-liter bottles ginger ale

5 cinnamon sticks

½ teaspoon freshly grated nutmeg or ground

Cranberries and apple wedges, peel left on, for garnish (optional)

Combine all of the ingredients in a large punch bowl. Garnish with the cranberries and apple wedges, if desired.

Banderillas

Banderillas are small, bite-size skewers, with tidbits of fish, olives, vegetables and the like. They can be served cold or grilled briefly to make them warm. Here are several Banderilla recipes.

SAUCE

- ½ cup minced fresh parsley
- ½ cup minced garlic cloves
- ½ cup finely minced dill pickle
- ½ cup olive oil

ANCHOVY SKEWERS

- 5 pitted green Spanish olives
- 5 1-inch pieces pickled herring
- 5 pieces pimiento
- 5 ½-inch-thick slices dill pickle
- 5 marinated pearl onions
- 5 rolled anchovies

TUNA SKEWERS

- 5 pitted green Spanish olives
- 5 ¼-inch-thick slices dill pickle
- 5 pieces pimiento
- 5 ¾-inch chunks solid white tuna meat

SHRIMP AND HAM SKEWERS

- 5 cooked shrimps, shelled, chilled
- 5 2-inch-long asparagus tips (cook in advance if served cold)
- 5 pieces sliced cured ham
- 5 small hard-boiled egg halves
- 16 to 20 6-inch wooden skewers

FOR SAUCE: Place the minced parsley, garlic and pickle in a food processor or blender. With the motor running, slowly add the oil and blend as smooth as possible.

FOR SKEWERS: Assemble the skewers, alternating ingredients, and serve the Banderillas, hot or cold, with the sauce.

Shrimp Puffs

MAKES 24 PUFFS

BITE-SIZE MORSELS OF SHRIMP IN A CHEESY *cloud are guaranteed favorites at any holiday gathering. It's a mild, chewy version of the popular Chinese shrimp toast. This versatile adaptation uses either a semisoft or hard cheese and can be mixed together in minutes.*

1 egg white

¼ cup grated Parmesan cheese

⅛ teaspoon salt

⅛ teaspoon paprika

Pinch cayenne pepper

½ cup mayonnaise

Crackers or toast rounds

12 shrimp, peeled, deveined, cut in half

Whip the egg white until stiff, then fold in the cheese, salt, paprika, cayenne pepper and mayonnaise. Mix gently, but well.

Place 1 to 2 teaspoons of the mixture onto the crackers. Place a half shrimp on top of each, then broil until light brown. Serve hot.

Mustard and Fruit Glazed Ham

SERVES 16

KUMQUATS AND PEARS are an interesting addition to the traditional pineapple and cherries that accompany a glazed ham. The colors and fruity flavors blend well with the saltiness of the meat. The leftovers make a heavenly hash or ham sandwich.

1 7- to 8-pound fully cooked bone-in ham (or larger, if needed)

1 cup firmly packed light brown sugar

¾ cup light corn syrup

⅓ cup prepared brown mustard

1 20-ounce can sliced pineapple

1 17-ounce can pear halves

9 to 10 preserved kumquats

9 to 10 maraschino cherries

2 small limes, thinly sliced

Preheat the oven to 375°F. Place the ham, fat side up, in a roasting pan. Bake, uncovered, for 2 to 2½ hours.

In a small, heavy saucepot, combine the brown sugar, corn syrup and mustard. Cook over low heat, stirring occasionally, until the sugar is dissolved and the mixture comes to a boil. Remove from the heat and stir in the fruit (except for the limes). Allow to soak for 2 hours.

Remove the skin from the ham and score 1-inch diamonds in the fat. Brush on about ¼ cup of the fruit syrup. Bake for 15 minutes. Arrange the pineapple slices, pears, kumquats and cherries onto the ham, securing them with toothpicks. Use any leftover fruit to garnish the platter. Brush the ham with ¼ cup more syrup and bake for another 15 minutes, or until nicely glazed and a meat thermometer reaches 130°F. Decorate with twisted lime slices.

Raspberry Glazed Turkey

SERVES 16

MAKE THIS GORGEOUS ROASTED TURKEY the star of your open house buffet table. Basting with a raspberry jam-flavored glaze, spiced with a dash of Dijon-style mustard, adds a beautiful garnet finish to the roast, while its fruity, zesty flavor pairs well with the turkey.

½ cup seedless raspberry jam

⅓ cup plus another ½ cup raspberry vinegar or raspberry liqueur

¼ cup Dijon-style mustard

1 teaspoon grated orange peel

½ teaspoon thyme

1 10-pound turkey

In a small mixing bowl, whisk together the first 5 ingredients.

Roast the turkey for 3 hours in a preheated 325°F oven, until an internal temperature of 180°F is reached. During the last hour of cooking, baste the bird with the glaze every 10 minutes. Remove the turkey from the oven and allow it to rest for at least 20 minutes before carving.

Rice with Caramelized Onion, Brandy and Red Bell Pepper

SERVES 20

USING MINUTE RICE makes fast work of this risotto-like side dish. Any number of vegetables and even cheese can be added to this recipe, making it a great dish for using up leftovers. It can also be served in a mold or as a main course.

¼ cup olive oil

3 medium onions, diced

1 tablespoon rosemary

½ teaspoon salt

¼ cup brandy

2 large red bell peppers, seeded, cut into 2-inch-long strips

5 garlic cloves, minced

½ teaspoon freshly grated nutmeg or ground

5 cups Minute Rice

4 cups vegetable or chicken broth

Freshly ground pepper to taste

In a large, heavy skillet, heat half of the oil over medium heat. Add the onions and rosemary. Stir frequently and cook until the onions are limp and nicely browned. Stir in the salt and brandy and set aside and keep warm.

Under a preheated broiler, cook the red bell pepper strips until they are cooked through and slightly browned, about 7 minutes. Set aside and keep warm.

Heat the remaining olive oil in a heavy-bottomed saucepan or Dutch oven. Sauté the garlic for 1 minute. Add the rice and nutmeg and stir to coat the grains. Add the broth ½ cup at a time, stirring almost constantly and waiting until the liquid is almost completely absorbed before adding more.

When the rice is about done, stir in the onion mixture, bell pepper strips and ground pepper. Serve immediately.

Baby Carrots with Mustard and Parsley

SERVES 20

BABY CARROTS WITH THEIR TOPS are beautiful and tender, but not always easy to find. Small, pretrimmed carrots can be bought in grocery stores by the bag. Using these carrots makes preparing this recipe for a crowd easy work. The brown sugar and mustard spices them up nicely.

5 pounds baby carrots

1 cup (2 sticks) unsalted butter

½ cup dark brown sugar

⅓ cup coarse mustard

Salt to taste

¼ cup finely chopped fresh parsley

Place the baby carrots in a large pot filled with salted water. Bring to a boil and cook until they are tender, about 5 minutes. Drain and cover with a cloth to keep them warm.

In a large sauté pan, melt the butter and sugar. Add the mustard and stir to combine well. Add the carrots in manageable batches and sauté over high heat for 3 minutes. Remove to a warm serving dish, sprinkle with the salt and parsley and toss well.

Bûche de Nöel

HERE IS AN OPPORTUNITY to become as creative and whimsical as you'd like. A Bûche de Nöel is made to look like a log (see photo on page 41), in honor of the glowing hearth of the Christmas season, and it can be decorated to any degree. Make meringue mushrooms sprinkled with cocoa, or chocolate leaves shaped like holly, or collect real leaves and spray them with gold or silver paint.

FOR CAKES

1	cup cake flour, sifted
1½	teaspoons baking powder
½	teaspoon salt
8	eggs, room temperature
1½	cups sugar
6	ounces unsweetened chocolate
2	teaspoons vanilla extract
¼	cup strong coffee
1	quart heavy cream
1	teaspoon vanilla extract
9	ounces unsweetened chocolate
½	cup unsalted butter
	Cocoa
¾	cup heavy cream
1	tablespoon vanilla extract
½	teaspoon salt
6	cups confectioner's sugar

FOR MERINGUE MUSHROOMS

2	egg whites
¼	teaspoon cream of tartar
½	cup sugar
2	tablespoons cocoa
¼	confectioners sugar
1	tablespoon water

FOR CAKES: Preheat the oven to 400°F. Line the bottom of 2 jelly roll pans with waxed paper. Sift together the flour, baking powder and salt. Set aside.

In a large bowl of an electric mixer, beat the eggs until they are foamy. Gradually add the sugar while continuing to beat at slow speed. Return to high speed and beat until the mixture is thick.

Melt the 6 ounces of chocolate and mix with the 2 teaspoons vanilla extract and the coffee. Add this to the egg mixture. Gently fold in the dry ingredients until just blended. Pour the batter into the prepared pans and smooth out, making sure it is even and reaches the corners.

Bake for 12 to 14 minutes, until the cakes spring back when lightly touched.

Lay flat 2 clean, linen dishtowels and sprinkle them with cocoa. Invert the cakes onto each towel. Peel off the waxed paper. Trim any crispy edges. Starting at the narrow end, roll up the cake and the towel. Allow to cool completely.

In a large bowl of an electric mixer, beat the 1 quart heavy cream and the 1 teaspoon vanilla extract until stiff.

Melt the 9 ounces of chocolate and the butter and mix well. Allow the mixture to cool to room temperature. Add the ¾ cup cream, 1 tablespoon vanilla extract and the salt. Gradually add the confectioner's sugar and beat well.

When the cakes are cool, unroll and remove the towels. Spread ¾ inch of whipped cream over each cake, leaving ½ inch around the edges. Reroll, being sure the cakes are resting with the seam sides down, and cover with plastic wrap. Refrigerate for an hour.

FOR MERINGUE MUSHROOMS: Preheat the oven to 200°F. Line two baking sheets with plain brown or parchment paper. In a small bowl, using an electric mixer, beat the egg white until foamy, about 5 to 7 minutes. Beat in the cream of tartar and then gradually, the sugar. When the whites are glossy and stiff, scrape ⅔ of them into a pastry bag fitted with a ½-inch opening. Pipe 1½-inch circles onto one of the baking sheets, 1-inch apart. With a damp finger, smooth out the tops. Place the cocoa in a fine sieve and sprinkle lightly over the "caps."

Place the remaining whites in the pastry bag and pipe out an equal amount of ½-inch cones which will become the stems. Place the meringues in the preheated oven and bake for 1 hour. Turn off the oven, gently lift each cap and using your finger, make a small indent in the smooth bottom. Return the caps to the baking sheet and place in the slowly cooling oven, along with the stems, for another 2 hours.

After 2 hours, remove the meringues from the oven and cool on a rack. Place the confectioners sugar in a small mixing bowl and add the water, a teaspoon at a time, stirring until a thick paste forms. When they are completely cool, place a dab of the confectioners sugar paste in the hollow of each cap. Insert the 'stem' and place the mushroom on a flat surface. Allow to set for ½ hour before using.

Uncover the cakes and cut each end at a diagonal. Save the end pieces for the branches. Place the cakes on serving platters. Spread the chocolate frosting over the cakes and score with a fork or a wide-toothed comb to resemble the bark of a tree. Place the removed wedges from the ends onto the sides of the cakes. Cover with frosting and swirl the frosting on the round part to resemble a cut-off branch. Dust the entire cake with confectioner's sugar to resemble snow. Top the logs with meringue mushrooms.

Italian Christmas Eve Dinner FOR 8

Stracciatella

Pan-Roasted Salmon
   with Citrus-Balsamic
   Vinaigrette

Fagioli alla Toscana

Broccoli Rabe Sautéed
   with Garlic

Chocolate Semifreddo

Coffee Amaretto

Stracciatella

SERVES 8

ITALIAN COMFORT FOOD AT ITS FINEST. The light, delicate flavors and appealing aroma of chicken stock in this delicious pasta soup make it appealing to all ages and a festive way to start a family meal. Be ready to serve it immediately once the egg and nutmeg are whisked into the broth.

5   cups chicken stock

1   teaspoon salt

½   cup *tripolini* (smallest bow-tie pasta)

2   eggs, beaten
    Dash freshly grated nutmeg or ground

4   tablespoons shredded Parmesan
    cheese

2   tablespoons chopped fresh parsley

In a large saucepot, bring the stock and salt to a boil. Add the pasta, lower the heat and simmer about 10 to 15 minutes, until the pasta is *al dente*. Mix together the eggs and nutmeg and add to the stock while stirring with a whisk. Ladle into bowls. Sprinkle with the cheese and parsley and serve immediately.

Pan-Roasted Salmon with Citrus-Balsamic Vinaigrette

SERVES 8

AN IDEAL MAIN DISH FOR A LATE EVENING holiday supper, beautiful pink salmon fillets enhanced with a savory, sweet citrus sauce are surprisingly easy and fast to prepare. Choose a good-quality balsamic vinegar to enjoy the full flavor of this dense, aromatic liquid. Combine the sauce ingredients in advance to speed the preparation process even more.

VINAIGRETTE

1½ cups fresh orange juice

1 cup balsamic vinegar

¼ cup extra-virgin olive oil

2 anchovy fillets, very finely minced (optional)

¼ cup finely minced onions

4 teaspoons coarsely chopped parsley

4 teaspoons coarsely chopped basil

4 teaspoons coarsely chopped mint

4 teaspoons finely minced orange zest

¼ teaspoon kosher salt

Freshly ground pepper to taste

1 teaspoon arrowroot

SALMON

8 6-ounce skinless salmon fillets

Coarse salt to taste

Freshly ground pepper to taste

¼ cup olive oil

FOR VINAIGRETTE: Combine all of the ingredients for the vinaigrette in a jar. Cover tightly and shake vigorously. Set aside.

FOR SALMON: Preheat the oven to 450°F. Season the salmon with salt and pepper to taste. In a roasting pan large enough to hold all of the fillets, heat the oil over high heat. Place the salmon, original skin side down, in the pan and transfer it to the oven to cook for 8 to 10 minutes, until medium-rare or desired doneness. Transfer the salmon onto a warm serving platter while finishing the vinaigrette.

Pour any of the juices from the roasting pan into a skillet. Add the jar of vinaigrette ingredients. Bring to a boil and simmer for a minute until it thickens slightly. Spoon the vinaigrette over the salmon and serve immediately.

Fagioli alla Toscana

SERVES 8

FAGIOLI, OR BEANS, ARE A STAPLE in Italian cooking. They add protein when combined with rice and they come in a myriad of colors and shapes. These white, broad beans, when sprinkled with sage, have a hearty flavor without being too filling.

32 ounces canned white beans

1 cup fresh sage leaves

2 teaspoons minced garlic

¼ cup olive oil

1 teaspoon salt

Freshly ground pepper to taste

Drain the beans and place them with the sage, garlic and olive oil in a medium saucepot. Add enough water to cover the beans. Bring to a boil and then lower the heat until the beans simmer gently. Cook until the mixture begins to thicken slightly, about 15 minutes. Season with the salt and pepper.

Broccoli Rabe Sautéed with Garlic

SERVES 8

ITALIAN COOKS ARE PARTICULARLY FOND of this leafy green vegetable, sometimes called "rapini," "rape" or "broccoletti di rape." Related to both the cabbage and turnip families, it has six- to nine-inch stalks with tiny clusters of broccoli-like buds and a nutty, slightly bitter flavor all its own.

2 large bunches broccoli rabe (about 3 pounds)

¼ cup olive oil

6 garlic cloves, sliced

Coarse salt to taste

Wash the broccoli rabe and remove the thickest parts of the stems. Chop coarsely. In a large pot with high sides, heat the oil over medium heat. Add the garlic and just as it begins to brown, add the broccoli rabe. Mix well and cover. Cook until the greens are wilted, about 5 minutes.

Place in a warm serving bowl, sprinkle with the salt and mix well.

Chocolate Semifreddo

A CLASSIC PAIRING OF CHOCOLATE AND ALMOND distinguishes this chilled dessert made with creamy ricotta cheese. Whether serving a crowd or just a few friends, it's ideal for a busy cook because it can be made in advance. Swirling a chocolate pattern over the surface gives a sophisticated touch. Serve with coffee flavored with a splash of amaretto to complete the meal in style.

¾ cup sugar

2 pounds ricotta cheese, drained

1 teaspoon almond extract

½ cup chocolate syrup

8 teaspoons chocolate syrup

Place the first 4 ingredients in the bowl of a food processor. Puree until mixed well and smooth.

Pour the mixture into 8 individual 4-ounce glasses or a 2-quart decorative serving bowl. Drizzle a teaspoon of the remaining syrup onto the surface of each cup or all of it onto the surface of the bowl. With a small knife or toothpick, swirl the chocolate through the ricotta to make a decorative effect.

Cover and chill for at least 2 hours or overnight.

CHRISTMAS BREAKFAST FOR 4 TO 6

Apricot Oat Bran Muffins

Sour Cream Pancakes

Omelets

Juices and Coffee

Apricot Oat Bran Muffins

MAKES 6 LARGE MUFFINS

THESE ARE NOT ONLY FLAVORFUL, but also low-fat and very healthy. They can be made ahead and frozen. Alone, with just a warm drink, they make a perfect breakfast. A coulis is a cooked or fresh fruit sauce which is used as a condiment. It can be sweet or savory according to need. This spicy combination is wonderful with muffins. Increase the brown sugar if you want it sweeter or add a tablespoon of balsamic or red wine vinegar to make it more like a chutney.

MUFFINS

- Cooking spray
- 2 cups oat bran
- ¼ cup packed brown sugar
- 1 tablespoon baking powder
- 2 egg whites
- 1 cup buttermilk
- ⅓ cup molasses
- 1 large apple, peeled, cored, grated
- ¾ cup finely chopped dried apricots

COULIS

- ¼ cup unsalted butter
- 3 large red apples, cored, cut into ½-inch wedges
- ¼ teaspoon ground cloves
- ¼ teaspoon freshly grated nutmeg or ground
- ½ teaspoon ground ginger
- 1 teaspoon dark brown sugar
- 1 tablespoon currants

FOR MUFFINS: Preheat the oven to 400°F. Spray a muffin pan with cooking spray.

In a large bowl, stir together the oat bran, brown sugar and baking powder. Make a well in the center of the mixture. Set aside. In a small mixing bowl, beat the egg whites until foamy. Stir in the buttermilk and molasses. Add the buttermilk mixture to the oat bran mixture and stir until just combined. Fold in the apple and apricots.

Spoon the batter into the muffin pan, filling each about ¾ full. Bake for 18 to 20 minutes or until a toothpick inserted in the center comes out clean. Cool for about 5 minutes, then remove from the pan and cool completely on a wire rack.

FOR COULIS: In a medium sauté pan, melt the butter over high heat. Add the apples and stir to coat them with the butter. Sprinkle the apples with the spices, sugar and currants. Continue to cook, stirring periodically, until the apples soften. Serve warm with the muffins or omelets.

Sour Cream Pancakes

SERVES 4 (MAKES ABOUT 16 PANCAKES)

START A FAMILY CHRISTMAS TRADITION by serving a special breakfast treat: sour cream pancakes. Rich and moist, these are no ordinary pancakes. Instead, they're embellished by adding sour cream, buttermilk and rolled oats to the batter. Served with fresh or frozen sliced peaches and blueberries, or exotic fruits in midwinter, they're a memorable way to begin Christmas day.

¾ cup flour

¼ cup quick-cooking rolled oats

1 tablespoon sugar

1 teaspoon baking powder

½ teaspoon baking soda

½ teaspoon ground cinnamon

¼ teaspoon salt

½ cup buttermilk

1 cup sour cream

1 egg

2 tablespoons unsalted butter, melted

Vegetable oil

Maple syrup, warmed

Sliced peaches, skins removed

Blueberries, stems removed

Grated orange peel

In a large bowl, stir together the flour, rolled oats, sugar, baking powder, baking soda, cinnamon and salt, mixing well.

In a large measuring cup, combine the buttermilk, sour cream, egg and melted butter. Beat until well mixed. Add the buttermilk mixture to the flour mixture and mix well to form a smooth batter.

For each pancake, pour about ¼ cup of the batter onto a hot griddle (greased with vegetable oil, if not non-stick). Cook until little bubbles appear on the tops of the pancakes, 3 to 5 minutes. Using a spatula, turn them and cook on the second side until both sides are equally browned, 1 to 2 minutes longer. Transfer to a warmed platter and keep them warm while you make more.

Drizzle the pancakes with the warmed maple syrup and top with the fruit and orange zest.

Omelets

MADE-TO-ORDER INDIVIDUAL OMELETS have great appeal when family or friends gather for a special holiday breakfast. Cultivating the skill to make omelets quickly and successfully is guaranteed to impress everyone. Practice with the ingredients outlined here, then try your own filling combinations.

12 **eggs, room temperature**
   Pinch salt
¼ cup unsalted butter
½ cup sun-dried tomatoes, dehydrated
½ cup grated Monterey Jack cheese
½ cup finely chopped green onions

Using 2 eggs for each omelet, break them into a small mixing bowl and sprinkle with a pinch of salt. Whisk with a fork until the yolks and whites are completely blended.

Over a medium flame, heat a nonstick, 7-inch pan with 2-inch sloping sides. Add a tablespoon of butter and swirl it around until it melts and is no longer frothing. Pour in the eggs and let them sit over the heat for just a few moments. With one hand, begin to tilt and gently shake the pan and with the other, using a fork, stir the eggs around so that they thicken at an even rate.

When the eggs are almost set through, add a tablespoon of each of the fillings, totaling no more than ½ cup. Using the fork, loosen the edges of the omelet and tilt the pan, allowing the omelet to fold over on itself. Take the pan away from the heat and hold it over the plate. Fold the omelet once more from the pan onto the plate. Serve at once.

Holiday Brunch FOR 16

Pumpkin Scones

Almond French Toast

Poached Eggs Florentine
with Mornay Sauce

Sausage and Potato Frittata

Cranberry Sparkle

Pumpkin Scones

MAKES ABOUT 30 SCONES

CINNAMON AND NUTMEG GO HAND IN HAND with pumpkin, as anyone who loves pumpkin pie can tell you. In this scone recipe, the combination is equally enticing, especially with crunchy chopped walnuts or pecans. If a holiday brunch is on the calendar, make the batter in advance and place scoopfuls onto baking sheets.

Freeze for two hours or more, then wrap the individual scoops in plastic wrap and freeze up to a month until ready to bake.

Cooking spray

4½ cups all-purpose flour

5 teaspoons baking powder

1 teaspoon ground cinnamon

½ teaspoon ground nutmeg or freshly grated

1 teaspoon salt

½ cup light brown sugar

½ cup unsalted butter, softened

2 cups canned pumpkin puree

1⅓ cups milk

2 cups chopped walnuts or pecans

Preheat the oven to 375°F. Grease 2 baking sheets with cooking spray.

In a large mixing bowl, combine the dry ingredients. Cut in the butter until it resembles coarse meal. Add the pumpkin, milk and nuts and stir until well mixed.

Using a ½ cup measure, scoop the batter into small rounds on the baking pans. Leave a space of about 2 inches between each scone. When both pans are used, put the remaining batter in the refrigerator until the first batch is finished baking.

Bake for 12 to 15 minutes, until the edges begin to brown. Remove to a cooling rack and repeat with the remaining batter.

Almond French Toast

SERVES 16

ALMOND FLAVORING COMBINED with crunchy sliced almonds adds novel flavor and texture to a dish that's always a winner when served at a family holiday brunch or after a marathon of opening presents. Use slightly stale, thick-sliced homemade or artisan bread for the best results. Thicker slices aren't as likely to fall apart when moved from the batter onto the griddle.

12 large eggs

2 teaspoons almond extract

2 teaspoons ground cinnamon

½ teaspoon ground nutmeg or freshly grated

¼ cup amaretto

3 cups half-and-half or milk

6 to 8 tablespoons unsalted butter

32 slices bread

2 cups thinly sliced almonds

Confectioner's sugar

Maple syrup, warmed

In a medium mixing bowl, beat the eggs. Whisk in the almond extract, ground cinnamon, nutmeg, amaretto and half-and-half.

Melt about ½ tablespoon of butter in a heavy skillet or griddle over medium-high heat and spread it around. Dip the bread, piece by piece, in the egg mixture until just barely soaked through. Cook until browned on one side, 2 to 3 minutes, then before flipping, sprinkle with almond slices. Flip and cook until the other side is nicely browned. Continue with all of the slices, adding butter as needed. Set each piece in shingle fashion on a large platter, keeping them warm in the oven as you cook. Sprinkle with confectioner's sugar and serve with warm maple syrup and butter.

Poached Eggs Florentine with Mornay Sauce

SERVES 16

A TRADITIONAL BÉCHAMEL SAUCE *of flour, butter and milk is enriched with eggs and flavored with Swiss or Gruyere cheese to make a creamy mornay sauce. Generously spooned over poached eggs served on a bed of wilted spinach and topped with browned breadcrumbs and cheese, this is a sophisticated brunch classic everyone will enjoy.*

MORNAY SAUCE

- ¼ cup butter or margarine
- ¼ cup all-purpose flour
- 1 tablespoon chicken broth
- Dash ground nutmeg or freshly grated
- Dash red pepper
- 4 cups half-and-half
- 1 cup shredded Swiss or Gruyere cheese

EGGS

- 32 eggs (can be done in an egg poacher or a skillet)
- 2¾ cups frozen spinach, thawed, drained
- 1 cup grated Parmesan cheese
- ½ cup breadcrumbs

FOR MORNAY SAUCE: In a small, heavy saucepot, melt the butter over medium heat. Add the flour, broth, nutmeg and red pepper. Cook over low heat, stirring constantly, until the roux begins to look runny. Using a wire whisk, stir in the half-and-half. Heat to boiling, stirring constantly. Add the cheese and stir until it is thoroughly melted.

Spread the spinach on a large, ovenproof serving platter and place in a 200°F oven while you cook the eggs.

FOR EGGS: In a large, wide skillet, poach the eggs until they are just opaque. Transfer them to the bed of spinach. Pour a few tablespoons of the mornay sauce over each egg, then sprinkle with the Parmesan and breadcrumbs. Turn the oven to broil and place the platter under the flame for 2 to 3 minutes or until the cheese melts and the breadcrumbs begin to brown.

Sausage and Potato Frittata

SERVES 16

FRITTATAS ARE SERVED AS TRADITIONAL Spanish bar food. Like many ethnic dishes, it's found its way into the American culinary mainstream and is being duplicated by home cooks who find it easy to make as an alternative to quiche. In this version, Italian sausage pairs deliciously with bell peppers and potatoes. Serve at room temperature with buttered corn tortillas.

1½ pounds sweet Italian sausage

2 potatoes, peeled, thinly sliced

12 eggs

½ teaspoon salt

1 tablespoon chopped fresh parsley

1 red bell pepper, seeded, diced

1 tablespoon olive oil

Preheat the oven to broil. In a large, ovenproof skillet, brown the sausage over medium-high heat. Remove the meat from the pan and drain on paper towels. Using the rendered fat from the sausage, cook the potatoes over medium heat until they begin to brown.

While the potatoes are cooking, beat the eggs in a large bowl. Add the browned sausage, potatoes, salt, parsley and the bell pepper. Mix well.

Heat the oil in the skillet over medium-high heat and tip the pan in a circular motion to spread the oil up the edges. Add the egg mixture and cook, shaking the skillet periodically, until the edges begin to bubble, about 3 to 5 minutes. Place the frittata under the broiler. Cook for 5 minutes or until the eggs begin to brown. As soon as it starts to brown, turn off the broiler and let the frittata remain in the closed oven for 10 minutes. Remove from the oven and allow to cool to room temperature before cutting into wedges and serving.

Cranberry Sparkle

MAKES 20 SERVINGS

THIS IS A THIRST QUENCHING COMBINATION to drink at any time. It is also very pretty with thin slices of oranges floating in the glass. At brunch it is a nice change from straight orange juice— but healthier than a mimosa!

1 quart cranberry juice cocktail

1 quart seltzer water or club soda

1 pint orange juice

1 orange, thinly sliced crosswise, then quartered

2 cinnamon sticks

In a decorative pitcher, combine the first 3 ingredients. Float the orange slices and cinnamon sticks on top.

CHRISTMAS FEAST FOR 8

Prosciutto with
Warm Wilted Greens

Beef Tenderloin
with Port-Rosemary Sauce

Pommes à la Dauphinoise

Spinach Sautéed
with Garlic

Christmas Pudding
with Hard Sauce

Irish Coffee

Prosciutto with Warm Wilted Greens

SERVES 8

VINEGAR AND SALT—from the vinaigrette and Prosciutto—expand the rich flavor of the leafy green vegetables. This is a healthy, savory start to a meal.

GREENS

9 large handfuls (about 4 pounds) greens (such as combination of kale, broccoli rabe, beet tops and chard)

⅓ cup olive oil

VINAIGRETTE

3 garlic cloves

⅓ cup red wine vinegar

¾ cup extra-virgin olive oil

Salt and freshly ground pepper to taste

24 very thin slices prosciutto

FOR GREENS: Go through the greens, removing any tough stalks. Chop coarsely and mix them together.

Pour the oil into a large, heavy skillet, and add just enough greens to fill the pan. Add a little water over the greens, cover and cook over medium-high heat. When the first batch has wilted, add more greens. Stir, cover and continue to cook, adding more greens as they wilt. When they are all wilted, check that they are tender and let them cool.

With your hands, squeeze out the liquid. Place the greens in a large mixing bowl.

FOR VINAIGRETTE: Peel and mash the garlic. Add the vinegar, then beat in the oil with a fork. Add any salt and pepper that is desired.

Toss the greens with the vinaigrette to coat evenly. Form mounds on each plate and surround with 3 pieces of prosciutto. Serve warm or cold.

Beef Tenderloin with Port-Rosemary Sauce

SERVES 8

THIS IS A TRULY ELEGANT BEEF RECIPE. The ingredients create a balance of sweet and savory from the butter and rosemary, both of which are heightened by the shallots, Port and red wine. Try to buy the best-quality aged beef, as the sauce does not mask the flavor of the meat.

SAUCE

- 2 tablespoons unsalted butter
- ¾ cup minced shallots
- 2 cups dry red wine
- 1½ cups port
- 2 cups beef broth
- 1 rosemary sprig or 1 teaspoon dried

BEEF

- 2 tablespoons olive oil
- 8 1-inch thick beef tenderloin slices
  Salt and freshly ground pepper
- ⅓ cup unsalted butter, chilled
- 2 teaspoons chopped fresh rosemary or ½ teaspoon dried, crumbled

FOR SAUCE: In a large, heavy skillet over medium-high heat, melt the butter. Add the shallots and sauté until tender. Stir in the wine and Port. Boil for 5 minutes. Add the broth and rosemary and boil until the liquid is reduced to 1 cup. Strain and set aside.

FOR BEEF: In a large, heavy skillet, heat the oil over medium-high heat. Season the beef with salt and pepper. Cook the beef in the skillet to the desired doneness, about 4 minutes per side for medium-rare. Transfer the beef to a serving platter and keep warm.

Add the sauce to the skillet in which you cooked the beef. Bring to a boil and scrape any brown bits into the sauce. Gradually add the butter, whisking until just melted. Do not allow the sauce to boil. Stir in the chopped rosemary. Season to taste with salt and pepper. Spoon the sauce over the beef and serve.

Pommes à la Dauphinoise

THESE ARE POTATOES SCALLOPED in the French manner. They are very quick and easy to pre-pare and are truly delicious and aromatic. The foods that come from the mountainous province of the Dauphine region in France are robust and are meant to fill you. The cheeses used in such cooking are chosen because they become creamy when heated, not stringy.

1   garlic clove

2   tablespoons unsalted butter

2¼   pounds potatoes, peeled, thinly sliced

1½   cups grated Swiss or Gruyere cheese

⅓   cup unsalted butter, cut into small chunks

½   cup light cream

    Salt and freshly ground pepper to taste

Preheat the oven to 400°F. Rub the bottom and sides of a baking dish with the garlic and then the 2 tablespoons of butter. Spread half of the potatoes in the bottom of the dish, sprinkle with half of the cheese and dot with half of the diced butter. Then do the second layer in the same way, on top of the first, with the remaining potatoes, cheese and butter. Pour the cream around the edges of the pan and then sprinkle with the salt and pepper. Cook in the oven for 30 to 40 minutes, until the potatoes are tender and the cheese is slightly browned on top.

Spinach Sautéed with Garlic

SERVES 8

NOT ONLY IS SPINACH readily available throughout the winter season, it is nutritious and easily prepared. The most difficult part of preparing spinach is being sure to get out all of the sand in which it grows. Soak the leaves in a large bowl of water and lift them out to dry on paper towels—this is important since pouring through a colander will simply dump the sand back onto the spinach. Rinse a couple of times to be sure you've got it completely clean.

5 pounds fresh spinach

4 tablespoons olive oil

3 garlic cloves, minced

1 teaspoon salt

Rinse the spinach well. Since spinach is so bulky when it is raw, you will probably need to do this in 2 batches.

In a wide pot, put 2 tablespoons of the olive oil and half of the garlic and sauté over medium heat for 1 minute. Add half of the spinach, stir and cover so that it will steam for 3 to 5 minutes. Remove the spinach to a warm bowl and repeat with the remaining oil, garlic and spinach. Toss with the salt.

Christmas Pudding with Hard Sauce

MAKES 2 PUDDINGS, SERVING 8 TO 10

CHRISTMAS PUDDING, which is also known as plum pudding, is traditionally made at least a month before Christmas and allowed to mellow in the refrigerator. It can, however, be made in as little time as one week before serving and stored in the refrigerator.

PUDDING

- 1 cup raisins
- 1 cup currants
- ¾ cup chopped mixed candied fruit peels
- ¼ cup brandy
- ¼ cup orange juice
- 2 cups all-purpose flour
- 1 tablespoon baking powder
- ½ teaspoon salt
- ½ teaspoon ground cloves
- ½ teaspoon ground cinnamon
- ½ teaspoon ground nutmeg or freshly grated
- 1 cup breadcrumbs
- 1 cup dark brown sugar
- ½ cup unsulphured molasses
- 2 cups (about 1 pound) grated beef suet (ask your butcher or meat department for suet)
- 1 cup peeled finely chopped tart apple
- 3 eggs, lightly beaten

HARD SAUCE

- 1 cup (2 sticks) unsalted butter, softened
- 1 cup confectioner's sugar
- ½ cup brandy, room temperature
- ⅛ teaspoon salt

FOR PUDDING: In a large bowl, mix the fruits, rinds, brandy and orange juice. Soak for a half hour. Sift together the flour, baking powder and spices. Add to the fruit mixture and stir in the remaining ingredients.

Butter 2 1-quart, heatproof glass or ceramic bowls or molds. Pour the mixture evenly into the bowls and cover with waxed paper and then 2 layers of aluminum foil. Steam each pudding separately. Place on a rack in a large pot and surround with water halfway up the bowl. Cover and steam for 3 hours. Allow to cool, and store in refrigerator.

FOR HARD SAUCE: Cream the butter and sugar until light and fluffy. Slowly add ¼ cup brandy and salt. Chill well before serving.

An hour before serving, reheat the pudding by steaming in the same way as it was cooked. Unmold onto a platter. Immediately before serving, darken the dining room, pour the remaining ¼ cup brandy over the pudding and light with a match. Serve with a dollop of the hard sauce or vanilla ice cream.

COUNTRY CHRISTMAS SUPPER FOR 12

Butternut Squash Soup

Buttermilk Biscuits

Pork Medallions with
Mandarin Oranges
and Cranberries

Roasted Root Vegetables

Crisp Potato Galette

Serious Pecan Pie

Hot Mocha

Butternut Squash Soup

SERVES 12

CONSIDERED BY SOME TO BE the king of squashes, mellow butternut squash stars in this hearty pureed soup that's a delicious beginning to any meal. Accented by salt, pepper, thyme and a dash of ground coriander, it's perfect fare for cold winter days.

2 medium onions, chopped

⅛ teaspoon white pepper

¼ teaspoon ground coriander

¼ cup unsalted butter

1 quart chicken broth

2 pounds butternut squash, peeled, seeded, cut into 1-inch cubes

4 pears, peeled, sliced

2 teaspoons chopped fresh thyme or ½ teaspoon dried

2 cups heavy whipping cream

2 thinly sliced unpeeled pears for garnish

1 cup chopped pecans for garnish

In a large heavy pot with a lid, cook the onions, white pepper and coriander in the butter, stirring frequently until they are translucent and tender. Add the broth, squash, peeled pears and thyme. Heat to boiling, reduce to a simmer, cover and cook for 12 to 15 minutes, until the squash is tender.

Working in manageable-size batches, puree the soup in a food processor or blender. Transfer it into another container. When all the soup has been pureed, return it to the pot. Add the cream. Heat, stirring frequently, until hot. Garnish with the sliced pears and pecans.

Buttermilk Biscuits

MARRIAGES HAVE BEEN MADE because of the flakiness and tenderness of homemade biscuits! While best served freshly baked and piping hot, busy cooks can make them a day or two ahead, then freeze and reheat them just before serving. However you prepare them, buttermilk biscuits turn any meal into "comfort food."

4	cups all-purpose flour
2	tablespoons baking powder
1	teaspoon baking soda
1	teaspoon salt
2	cups buttermilk
⅓	cup corn oil
2	tablespoons vanilla extract

Preheat the oven to 425°F. In a large bowl, mix together the dry ingredients. Make a well in the center and add the wet ingredients. Mix well and turn onto a lightly floured board. Knead gently a few times and roll out to ½-inch thickness. Cut out round or decorative shapes with a cutter and place on a greased baking sheet.

Bake for 10 to 12 minutes or until they begin to brown. Serve warm in a basket lined with a cloth napkin.

Pork Medallions with Mandarin Oranges and Cranberries

SERVES 12

SERVING PORK IN MEDALLIONS, a term referring to meat cut into round or oval shapes, is more unusual than beef medallions, but has the same appeal. Medallions cook quickly and make an elegant plate presentation. This colorful preparation, with the flavors of sweet, tangy citrus and cranberries, pairs well with "the other white meat."

6 tablespoons unsalted butter

⅓ cup olive oil

24 good-size pork medallions (from pork tenderloin)

Salt and freshly ground pepper to taste

6 garlic cloves, minced

1 tablespoon chopped fresh rosemary or 1 teaspoon crumbled dried

1 teaspoon ground cinnamon

⅛ teaspoon ground cloves

⅓ cup dark brown sugar

1 33-ounce can mandarin orange sections, liquid reserved

1½ cups Marsala wine

1½ cups whole cranberries or whole cranberry sauce

Rosemary sprigs for garnish

In a large, heavy sauté pan over medium-high heat, melt half of the butter in all of the olive oil. Season the pork with salt and pepper. Working in batches so as not to crowd the pan, sauté the pork for 10 to 12 minutes on each side, until well browned and cooked through. Remove and keep warm in a 200°F oven.

Melt the remaining butter in the pan and add the garlic, rosemary, cinnamon, cloves, brown sugar and ⅓ cup of the mandarin orange liquid. Simmer, stirring for a few seconds, then add the Marsala and bring to a boil. Boil until the sauce is reduced by about half and thickened. Lower the heat to medium. Add the cranberries and cook until they burst, 1 to 2 minutes. Add the mandarin orange sections and salt and pepper to taste. Heat thoroughly and then spoon the sauce over the medallions. Garnish with the rosemary sprigs and serve.

Roasted Root Vegetables

As a simple and healthful winter vegetable dish, this one can't be beat. Roasting vegetables in a very hot oven produces a natural crust while maintaining the internal juices and bringing out the natural sweetness. If you can't find one of the squash or root vegetables listed here, simply substitute more of another one.

1 pound parsnips, peeled,
   cut into 1-inch pieces

1 pound celery root, peeled,
   cut into 1-inch pieces

1 pound rutabaga, peeled,
   cut into 1-inch pieces

1 pound butternut or other firm squash,
   peeled, cut into 1-inch pieces

2 onions, coarsely chopped

4 garlic cloves, minced

¼ cup coarsely chopped fresh oregano
   or 2 tablespoons dried

⅔ cup olive oil

2 teaspoons coarse salt

1 teaspoon freshly ground pepper

Preheat the oven to 450°F.

In a large mixing bowl, toss together all of the ingredients until well mixed. Arrange them in a single layer in 2 glass baking dishes. Cover with foil. Roast for 30 to 40 minutes, stirring every 10 minutes, until the vegetables are soft and golden at the edges. Serve hot.

Crisp Potato Galette

SERVES 12

FEW MORE UNIVERSALLY APPEALING dishes can be imagined than fried potatoes. Prepared here in flat, round cakes, they join the infinite variations of galettes made in kitchens since Roman times, and most likely before. The name itself is derived from the French word for a flat, round skipping stone. As an alternative to mashed or roasted potatoes, this version is beyond compare!

5 pounds baking potatoes, peeled, julienned

1 tablespoon chopped fresh thyme

1 teaspoon salt

½ teaspoon white pepper

1 cup olive oil

In a large bowl, combine the julienned potatoes, thyme, salt and pepper.

In a 12-inch, heavy skillet, heat about ¼ inch of the olive oil until it's very hot. Divide the potatoes into mounds that will flatten into 4-inch circles and place 2 or 3 of them in the pan at a time. Cook over medium heat until you can see them brown around the edges. Flip each one over and brown the other side. Remove to a warm oven while you cook the remaining potatoes.

Serious Pecan Pie

SERVES 12

A NUT NATIVE ONLY TO NORTH AMERICA, pecans have inspired some delightfully decadent desserts, including pecan pie. That noted, it must be said that there are pecan pies and then there are Pecan Pies. This is one of the latter in the traditional style—not too sweet or heavy, but satisfyingly rich with nuts throughout the filling. It's a natural with coffee or hot mocha (see recipe on page 83).

- 2 9-inch pie shells
- 2/3 cup unsalted butter, melted
- 1 1/3 cups packed brown sugar
- 6 eggs
- 2 cups dark corn syrup
- 2 1/2 cups broken or coarsely chopped pecans
- 2 tablespoons rum
- 1 teaspoon salt

Preheat the oven to 450°F. Bake the empty pie shells for 5 to 7 minutes. Remove and allow them to cool while preparing the filling. Reduce the oven temperature to 375°F.

In a large mixing bowl, using a wire whisk, cream the butter and brown sugar. Beat in the eggs, one at a time, and then the corn syrup. Stir in the pecans, rum and salt. Blend thoroughly. Pour the filling into the shells and bake at 375°F for 40 to 45 minutes. Serve warm with vanilla ice cream. This pie is also good cold, though much chewier.

Hot Mocha

SERVES 12

REMEMBER THOSE BLUSTERY WINTER afternoons as a kid when a cup of hot cocoa seemed like heaven? This is a sophisticated version made rich, dark and appealing by blending coffee with chocolate and adding a topping of whipped cream. Use Dutch-processed cocoa for even more intense flavor.

1 cup ground coffee

3 quarts milk

1 cup cocoa

1 cup sugar

¼ cup salt

   Whipped cream

In a large pot, combine all of the ingredients and bring to a boil. Quickly lower the heat and allow the mixture to barely simmer for 15 minutes. Strain through a double-layer piece of cheesecloth. Ladle into mugs and serve with a dollop of whipped cream.

Elegant Holiday Dinner FOR 12

Lobster Bisque

Mixed Green Salad
with Vinaigrette

Rosemary Roasted Turkey

Corn Bread Stuffing with
Cranberries and Pecans

Cauliflower and Broccoli
Timbales

Parsnips and Sweet Potato
Batons Flambéed
in Bourbon

Wassail

Flourless Chocolate Cake

Lobster Bisque

SERVES 12

SHELLFISH BISQUES FIRST STARTED appearing in the 17th century in Europe. New Englanders, who have always had an abundance of fresh shellfish at their disposal, adapted this soup as an elegant version of a chowder. This is a wonderful way to stretch a relatively small amount of lobster meat so that a large group can be served.

¾ cup unsalted butter

3 medium onions, chopped

3 garlic cloves, chopped

3 medium carrots, chopped

2 bay leaves

1 teaspoon thyme

3 lobster tails, meat removed, chopped, shells reserved

3 cups dry white wine

3 cups chopped tomatoes

6 cups fish or chicken stock

2 cups heavy cream

Salt and freshly ground pepper to taste

⅓ cup chopped fresh parsley

In a large saucepot over medium heat, melt the butter. Add the onions, garlic, carrots, bay leaves and thyme. Cook until the onions become translucent, stirring occasionally. Add the lobster shells and cook until they turn red. Add the wine and tomatoes and bring to a boil. Lower the heat and simmer for 5 minutes. Add the stock, bring to a boil, and again lower the heat to a simmer for 20 minutes. Remove the bay leaves and lobster shells.

Place the soup in batches in a blender or food processor and pulse until smooth. At this point the soup can be held in the refrigerator. Before serving, return the soup to a pot and bring to a boil. Add the chopped lobster meat and let the soup simmer for 5 minutes. Add the cream and heat through. Season with salt and pepper. Ladle into bowls and sprinkle with the parsley.

Rosemary Roasted Turkey

SERVES 12

THE CENTERPIECE OF A CHRISTMAS MEAL, a roasting turkey also fills your house with the aromas of what's to come. This turkey adds the lovely, spicy smell of rosemary. The sauce, made with the turkey drippings, will add an abundance of flavor to a juicy bird. A dry red wine, such as a Beaujolais Nouveau, gives the sauce a distinct flavor that accents the other seasonings in it.

TURKEY

1 8- to 12-pound turkey (1 pound uncooked per person)

⅓ cup olive oil

1 tablespoon garlic powder

2 teaspoons coarse salt

1 tablespoon freshly ground pepper

⅓ cup dried rosemary

SAUCE

Drippings from roasted turkey

2 cups chicken stock

2 cups Beaujolais Nouveau or dry red wine, ⅓ cup set aside

2 tablespoons cornstarch

½ teaspoon salt

Freshly ground pepper to taste

FOR TURKEY: Preheat the oven to 325°F. Rinse and dry the turkey. Place it on a rack in a large roasting pan. Drizzle the oil over the bird and rub it all over its skin. Sprinkle it with the garlic powder, salt and pepper. Crumble the rosemary all over the bird and at the cavity opening.

Place the turkey in the oven and roast for 3½ to 4½ hours (20 minutes per pound) or until the temperature at the thigh is 170°F. If the turkey is becoming too brown, cover it loosely with aluminum foil.

Remove the turkey from the oven and allow it to rest for 15 minutes before carving. Pour the drippings into a tall jar or pitcher and reserve for the sauce.

FOR SAUCE: Allow the turkey drippings to settle. Pour off the fat that rises to the top. Using a spoon, remove as much as possible. Strain through a sieve.

In a large saucepan, bring the drippings and stock to a boil. Add the 1⅔ cups of wine and continue to boil until it has reduced by half. Skim off the foam as it rises to the surface.

Dissolve the cornstarch into the remaining ⅓ cup of wine and gradually add to the drippings mixture, whisking continually. Lower the heat and simmer for 3 minutes. Season with the salt and pepper. Serve with the turkey in a heated sauceboat.

Corn Bread Stuffing with Cranberries and Pecans

SERVES 12

THE HOMEY QUALITY OF CORN BREAD, combined with the festive color of cranberries, makes this stuffing the perfect accompaniment to a Christmas turkey. Keeping leftover corn bread in the freezer for later use as a breading, croutons or stuffing is also a quick way to add flavor to any meal.

1 cup unsalted butter

3 garlic cloves, minced

1 cup chopped celery

½ teaspoon sage

½ teaspoon thyme

1 teaspoon salt

16 ounces corn bread, cubed, or corn bread stuffing mix

½ cup chicken stock

1 cup cranberries

1 cup chopped green onions

1 cup pecans

In a large sauté pan, melt ½ cup of the butter over medium heat. Add the garlic and cook for 1 minute. Add the celery and spices and cook for about 5 minutes, until the celery turns bright green. Add the remaining butter and when it is melted, add the corn bread, chicken stock, cranberries, green onions and pecans. Toss well.

Place the stuffing into a 2-quart baking pan, cover, and place in the oven with the turkey during the final 45 minutes of cooking.

Cauliflower and Broccoli Timbales

SERVES 12

CAULIFLOWER AND BROCCOLI ARE SUCH winter staples, it's fun to dress them up together and show that they too can have the elegance of asparagus or snow peas. These can be made well ahead and reheated in the microwave or oven.

2 small heads cauliflower

4 bunches broccoli, 3 florets set aside

1½ cups heavy cream

6 eggs

½ teaspoon salt

½ teaspoon white pepper

6 cherry tomatoes, halved, for garnish

Preheat the oven to 375°F. Steam the cauliflower in 2 inches of water until it is tender. Drain and cool. Do the same for the broccoli.

Whisk together the cream, eggs, salt and white pepper.

In a food processor, puree the cauliflower with ⅔ of the cream mixture. Spoon into 12 buttered, 6-ounce timbale molds ⅓ of the way up, and smooth the surface. Gently tap the molds on the counter to remove any air bubbles.

Chop the reserved broccoli florets and sprinkle them in a very thin layer over the cauliflower molds.

In a clean bowl of a food processor, puree the broccoli with the remaining cream mixture. Pour the puree over the chopped florets until the mold is ⅔ the way filled. Smooth the surface.

Place the molds in a baking pan and add enough boiling water to reach halfway up the sides of the molds.

Place in the oven and bake for ½ hour, or until a knife inserted in the middle of the timbale comes out clean.

Run a warm knife around the edge of each mold and invert onto a serving platter. Garnish with a cherry tomato half.

Parsnips and Sweet Potato Batons Flambéed in Bourbon

SERVES 12

Two LOWLY WINTER VEGETABLES show off their elegant side in this festive dish. The richness of caramelized sugar and the subtle bourbon flavor enhance the naturally sweet taste of parsnips and sweet potatoes—the delicious result makes all the chopping worth the effort.

1 pounds parsnips

4 pounds sweet potatoes

¼ cup unsalted butter

2 teaspoons dark brown sugar

½ teaspoon salt

⅓ cup bourbon, warmed

Peel the parsnips and sweet potatoes and cut them into 2-inch matchsticks. Melt the butter in a large sauté pan. Add the parsnips and the sweet potatoes and cook over medium heat for 5 minutes. Sprinkle with the brown sugar and salt. Cook the matchsticks evenly by shaking the pan every once in a while.

Turn the heat up to high and add the bourbon. Standing a little away from the pan, ignite the bourbon with a match. The flames will be high and fast but go ahead and shake the pan back and forth. That will settle down the flames and assure that all of the alcohol has burned off. Remove to a warm serving dish.

Wassail

LONG ASSOCIATED WITH WINTER FESTIVITIES and Christmas revels, this beverage takes its name from the old English salutation wishing a person good health when presenting them with a cup of drink. Enjoy the fragrant, spicy aroma as it simmers on the stovetop. For an adult version, add one half cup each brandy and rum, plus a can of ale.

4 to 5 sticks cinnamon

12 whole cloves

1 gallon apple cider

1½ cups brown sugar

½ cup lemon juice

2 lemons, sliced

Place the cinnamon and cloves in a spice bag or knotted handkerchief-size piece of cheesecloth, add the bag to the cider and boil for 5 minutes or so. Remove the spice bag and add the sugar, lemon juice and lemons. Boil for 5 minutes more. Serve hot.

Flourless Chocolate Cake

SERVES 12

THE MOST ELEGANT AND SATISFYING way to end a Christmas feast is with a soufflé-like choco-late cake surrounded by vibrant raspberry and creamy vanilla sauces. The tartness of the raspberries will heighten the flavor of the chocolate and the vanilla prevents it from tasting too rich.

CAKE

- 10 ounces semisweet chocolate
- 6 tablespoons unsalted butter
- 8 eggs, separated, room temperature
- 1 cup sugar
- 2 tablespoons framboise liqueur

RASPBERRY SAUCE

- 16 ounces frozen raspberries
- 2 tablespoons confectioner's sugar
- 1 tablespoon framboise liqueur

- 1 pint vanilla ice cream, melted
- Mint sprigs for garnish

FOR CAKE: Preheat the oven to 275°F. In a microwave, or the insert bowl of a double boiler, melt the chocolate and butter and stir until combined. Set aside.

In a small bowl of an electric mixer, beat the yolks and sugar with a whisk until the mixture is pale yellow in color and forms a ribbon when lifted from the bowl.

In a separate, clean bowl, beat the whites until they are stiff, but not to the point of being dry.

In a large mixing bowl, combine the chocolate and the yolk mixture. Add the framboise and mix well. Gently, using your hands, fold in the whites until completely combined.

Butter a 10-inch springform pan. Pour in the batter and cook for 2¼ hours. Gently remove the ring from the cake and allow to cool.

FOR SAUCE: In a small, heavy saucepot, heat the raspberries until they are soft and melted. Add the confectioner's sugar and stir to break up the berries. Bring to a boil, stirring, lower the heat and add the framboise. Cool slightly, and then strain through a sieve to remove the seeds.

Warm the sauce in a pot over low heat then pour it into a pitcher just before serving. Pour a dollop of raspberry sauce onto half of the plate. Allow the sauce to spread. On the other side of the plate, pour some of the melted ice cream. Allow it to spread. Cut a wedge of the cake and place it between the 2 sauces. Garnish with a small sprig of mint.

GIFTS FROM THE KITCHEN

Scottish Shortbread Cookies	Brandied Apricot Jam
Almond Brittle	Creole Jam
Christmas Crescents	Mint Jelly
Quick Molasses Cookies	Pear Chutney
Cranberry Chip Cookies	Cranberry Ketchup
Graham Cracker Crackle Cookies	Cranberry Chutney
Coffee Brownies	Tangerine-Fig Relish
Bourbon Balls	Chestnut Pieces in Syrup
Gateau Bourbon Spice Cake	Chocolate Sauce
Don Bowersox's Pumpkin Bread	Butterscotch Sauce
Banana Nut Bread	

$\mathcal{V}$isions of sugarplums dance in everyone's head during the holidays, and there's no better season for a bit of sweet indulgence. No matter if they're eight years old or eighty, when the gift is a homemade treat, the recipient's eyes always light up at the sight of mouthwatering cookies, a tantalizing cake or nut bread, to-die-for Bourbon Balls, a deep, dark chocolate sauce, or delectable fruit preserves. It's an exchange I thoroughly enjoy. I find as much pleasure in the giving as in the making. In this season of sharing, it's true that a gift from the kitchen is a heartfelt token of love and goodwill.

Among the suggestions here for Christmas gifts baked or made in the kitchen, you'll find tried and true favorites from my family. I inherited my love of cooking and delicious food from a line of outstanding home cooks, so the tradition of sharing homemade gifts from the kitchen was one I learned early on. You'll find my father Don's moist and perfectly spiced Pumpkin Bread (delicious toasted and buttered as a Christmas morning snack while undoing stockings). My mother, Marilee, contributed her dynamite recipe for Butterscotch Sauce— and I admit I haven't been able to improve upon it. All of us in the Bowersox clan confess to a sweet tooth, so there are very well-tested family recipes for Bourbon Balls and Almond Brittle.

I've included traditional Christmas sweets like Christmas Crescents and Banana Nut Bread. These are always a hit when there are children in the family and a good choice when you're not certain of taste preferences. But many of the selections here are more exotic than the standard cookies or fruitcake, so you can indulge your creative side in the kitchen, too. You'll find rich sauces and unusual condiments like Creole Jam, Tangerine-Fig Relish and Pear Chutney. These are surprisingly easy to make—even simpler than some holiday cookies—and provide a sparkling flavor accent to holiday main courses like roast beef, turkey or lamb.

All of the items here can be transported easily, as well as made in advance—some even months in advance—when time and the inclination allow. Preparing treats ahead helps keep the holiday stress level more manageable. I can say it's a pleasure and satisfaction to survey my pantry or freezer at the end of September and know I have "gifts in waiting" for the holidays when there will be so many other things to do on the calendar.

Whether the item you're making is sweet or savory, when fragrances of spices, dried fruits and chocolate drift through your kitchen, I guarantee that your creative spirit and your culinary senses will feel indulged. Without a doubt, Christmas is just the very best time of the year to make something we often don't find time for the rest of the year, and that pleasure is doubled when the treat becomes a gift.

Scottish Shortbread Cookies

MAKES 4 DOZEN COOKIES

SHORTBREAD CAN BE FOUND all over the British Isles, including of course, in Scotland. Traditional shortbread contains few ingredients, making proportions important, so be sure to measure carefully. Rounds of shortbread are often baked in decorative wooden molds, but this rich, buttery cookie tastes equally divine when the dough is formed by hand and baked into a flat disk.

¼ cup confectioner's sugar

¼ cup sugar

1¼ cups (2½ sticks) unsalted butter, chilled

2½ cups flour

Preheat the oven to 350°F. In a medium bowl, whisk together the sugars. In a second, larger bowl, cream the butter with the sugars until light and fluffy.

With your fingers, mix in the flour until the mixture holds together.

Measure 2 level teaspoons of the dough and knead each piece by flattening it between your palms and then rolling it into a 1-inch ball. Place each ball on a cookie sheet, flattening it with a cookie press, fork or the bottom of a glass lightly moistened with water. Bake for 45 minutes to 1 hour or until pale golden. Transfer to wire racks to cool.

Almond Brittle

MAKES 1½ POUNDS

It wouldn't be Christmas at the Bowersox residence without a supply of this buttery, almond-studded caramel candy on hand. It's definitely a family favorite! We use unblanched, slivered almonds rather than whole for easier munching. Plus, I recommend using a candy thermometer to ensure accurate cooking time and eliminate guesswork. Once cooled and broken, pack the brittle into airtight, decorative tins if you're shipping gifts, or use unusual glass or wicker containers for local friends.

2½   cups unblanched slivered almonds
¾   cup packed light brown sugar
⅔   cup light corn syrup
¼   cup water
¼   teaspoon salt
1   tablespoon unsalted butter
1   teaspoon vanilla extract
½   teaspoon almond extract

Preheat the oven to 300°F.

In a large, heavy skillet over medium flame, heat the almonds and stir gently until they begin to brown. As soon as they begin to brown, remove the almonds to a plate. Place in the oven.

In a heavy, 1½-quart saucepot, heat the brown sugar, corn syrup, water and salt to a boil. Brush down the sides of the pot with some water to make sure that no sugar crystals remain. Boil, without stirring, until a candy thermometer reads 290°F.

Butter a jelly roll pan and a metal spatula.

When the syrup is done, remove from the heat and add the almonds, butter, vanilla and almond extract. Stir well. Pour it onto the pan and spread with the spatula. Allow to cool.

Break up the brittle and put it into airtight containers. Allow the candy to mellow for a day before serving.

Christmas Crescents

MAKES ABOUT 7 DOZEN COOKIES

OFTEN CALLED VIENNESE CRESCENTS OR almond crescents, these delicate butter cookies hail from Austria and Bavaria where they are a must on every Christmas cookie tray. Their fragile texture enriched with finely chopped nuts and almond flavoring makes them irresistible. In this version, colored sugars are used instead of the traditional dusting of confectioner's sugar so that they'll sparkle in a gift basket.

1 cup (2 sticks) unsalted butter, softened

1¼ cups confectioner's sugar

1 egg yolk

1 teaspoon almond extract

¼ teaspoon salt

2 cups all-purpose flour

1 cup finely chopped pecans, almonds or walnuts

Colored sugar

Preheat the oven to 350°F.

In a large mixing bowl, working with a wooden spoon, combine the butter and confectioner's sugar until they are well blended and fluffy. Add the yolk, almond extract and salt. Beat until blended. Gradually add the flour and chopped nuts and beat until it is totally incorporated and a dough is formed.

Break off small handfuls of dough and roll between your palms into ½-inch ropes. Cut each rope into 2-inch lengths and shape into crescents, placing each crescent onto ungreased baking sheets as you form them. Sprinkle each crescent with the colored sugar.

Bake the crescents for 10 to 12 minutes or until the bottoms are light brown. The tops of the cookies should remain pale. Remove them to a wire rack to cool.

Quick Molasses Cookies

MAKES ABOUT 2½ DOZEN COOKIES

FROM MEDIEVAL TIMES and even earlier, seafaring merchants brought prized spices like cinnamon, cloves, nutmeg and ginger from India and Indonesia to Europe where they were used to prepare foods for the lavish midwinter feasts of wealthy nobles. These rolled, cut-out cookies carry on that legacy with their medley of spices and sassy molasses flavor.

Cooking spray
⅓ cup packed brown sugar
⅓ cup margarine
⅔ cup molasses
1 egg
2¾ cups all-purpose flour
2 teaspoons ground cinnamon
1 teaspoon ground ginger
1 teaspoon baking soda
1 teaspoon salt

Preheat the oven to 375°F. Lightly grease 2 cookie sheets with cooking spray.

In a large mixing bowl, combine the brown sugar, margarine, molasses and egg. Stir in the flour, cinnamon, ginger, baking soda and salt. Roll the dough to ¼-inch thick on a lightly floured surface. Cut into desired shapes with cookie cutters. Place about 1 inch apart on the cookie sheets. Bake for 7 to 8 minutes or until no indentation remains when touched. Remove to a wire rack to cool.

Cranberry Chip Cookies

MAKES ABOUT 5½ DOZEN COOKIES

A VARIATION ON THAT PERENNIAL American favorite, chocolate chip cookies, this novel version takes advantage of autumn's fresh cranberries for flavor, texture and visual appeal. Naturally tart cranberries are counterbalanced by semisweet chocolate, brown sugar and subtle orange flavors to create a sophisticated cookie that appeals to both adults and children— and even Santa! If you can't find fresh cranberries, try dried or frozen.

Preheat the oven to 375°F. Lightly grease 2 baking sheets with cooking spray.

In a large mixing bowl, combine the butter and sugars. Stir in the milk, orange juice and egg. Add the remaining ingredients and combine gently.

Drop the dough by rounded teaspoonfuls about 2 inches apart on the cookie sheets. Bake for about 10 to 12 minutes or until light brown. Cool on a wire rack.

Cooking spray

8 tablespoons (1 stick) unsalted butter, softened

1 cup sugar

¾ cup packed brown sugar

¼ cup milk

2 tablespoons orange juice

1 egg

3 cups flour

1 teaspoon baking powder

½ teaspoon salt

¼ teaspoon baking soda

2½ cups coarsely chopped cranberries

1 cup chopped nuts

½ cup semisweet chocolate chips

Graham Cracker Crackle Cookies

MAKES ABOUT 18 COOKIES

WHOLESOME GRAHAM CRACKER CRUMBS replace flour in this drop cookie that has a meringue base and is studded with chocolate chips. When baked, the flavor combination of graham crackers, chocolate and slightly chewy meringue is reminiscent of s'mores heated over a campfire—but these cookies are easier to eat and there's no risk of them falling into the flames.

1 large egg white

⅛ teaspoon cream of tartar

1¼ cups confectioner's sugar

2 tablespoons malted milk powder

½ cup finely crushed graham cracker crumbs

Flour

¼ cup semisweet chocolate chips

Preheat the oven to 375°F.

In a large bowl, mix the egg white, cream of tartar, sugar and malted milk powder. Beat with an electric mixer at high speed until thick and smooth. Stir in the graham cracker crumbs.

Drop the dough in 1½-teaspoon mounds 3 inches apart on a nonstick baking sheet that has been sprinkled with flour. Lightly press an equal amount of chocolate chips into each mound.

Bake until golden brown, about 7 minutes. Transfer to racks and let cool.

Coffee Brownies

MAKES 12 LARGE OR 20 SMALL BROWNIES

A VARIATION ON AMERICA'S all-time favorite bar cookie, this version will seduce espresso lovers and everyone else on your gift list. These glazed brownies are dense, rich and intense. Top with a scoop of premium vanilla ice cream and a splash of hot fudge sauce for a truly decadent dessert.

BROWNIES

- 8 ounces unsweetened chocolate, coarsely chopped
- 1¼ cups (2½ sticks) unsalted butter, softened
- ¼ cup finely ground espresso beans
- ½ teaspoon salt
- 2½ cups sugar
- 5 large eggs
- 1 teaspoon vanilla extract
- 1¼ cups flour
- 1 cup coarsely chopped pecans

GLAZE

- ¼ cup Kahlúa
- 1 teaspoon vanilla extract
- 1 tablespoon unsalted butter, softened
- 1 cup confectioner's sugar

FOR BROWNIES: Preheat the oven to 325°F. Butter and flour a 9 x 12-inch baking pan. Line the bottom with waxed or parchment paper. Butter and flour the paper.

In the top of a double boiler set over simmering water, combine the chocolate, butter, espresso and salt. Stir until smooth. Remove from the water and allow to cool.

In a large bowl, whisk together the sugar, eggs and vanilla until smooth. Add the melted chocolate mixture and stir until combined. Gently fold in the flour and pecans. Pour into the prepared pan, smoothing the top. Bake about 35 minutes, until a toothpick comes out clean.

FOR GLAZE: Whisk together the Kahlúa, vanilla and butter. Add the confectioner's sugar and beat until a smooth icing forms. Spread over the cooled brownies and let set for 1 hour before cutting into squares.

Bourbon Balls

THE CURRENT CRAZE NOTWITHSTANDING, truffles have nothing on this confection. Ground pecans, cocoa and crushed vanilla wafers serve as the base for these melt-in-your-mouth chocolate delights. For gift giving, place the Bourbon Balls in red and gold foil candy cups (smaller than baking cups) and present them in a decorative box or basket. Even guests who abstain from dessert won't be able to resist these sweets.

3 cups pecans

8 cups vanilla wafers

⅓ cup cocoa

3 cups confectioner's sugar

¾ cup bourbon

⅓ cup light corn syrup

1 cup confectioner's sugar

In the bowl of a food processor, working in batches, grind the pecans until they are fine but be careful not to make a paste. Remove to a large bowl. Do the same with the vanilla wafers and then add to the nuts.

Sift the cocoa and the 3 cups of confectioner's sugar onto the nut mixture. Combine well. Add the bourbon and corn syrup and mix well. Form into quarter-size balls and dredge in the remaining confectioner's sugar. Age for at least a week in the refrigerator.

Gateau Bourbon Spice Cake

MAKES 1 CAKE

HAILING FROM THE DEEP SOUTH, this cake recipe has been in my family for decades, if not generations. With a bow to pound cakes for inspiration, its assorted spices team up with bourbon to make a heady flavor combination, while buttermilk creates a light, open texture.

Be sure to use a good-quality bourbon for the richest taste because the flavor will linger even as the alcohol is baked off in the oven.

2 cups flour

1 tablespoon baking powder

1 teaspoon baking soda

1 teaspoon ground ginger

1 teaspoon ground cinnamon

½ teaspoon ground cardamom

½ teaspoon allspice

½ teaspoon ground cloves

¼ teaspoon salt

½ cup good-quality bourbon

¾ cup buttermilk

1 cup unsalted butter, softened

1¼ cups sugar

2 eggs

Confectioner's sugar

Preheat the oven to 350°F. Butter and flour a 10-inch cake pan.

Combine the dry ingredients and set aside. Combine the bourbon and buttermilk. With an electric mixer, cream the butter and sugar until light and fluffy. Add the eggs, one at a time, beating well between additions. Add about ¼ of the dry ingredients alternating with about ⅓ of the bourbon/buttermilk mixture. Keep alternating, beginning and ending with the dry ingredients.

Pour the cake batter into the prepared pan. Bake for 45 minutes or until a toothpick comes out clean. Cool 10 minutes in the pan, then remove to a cooling rack. Cool and dust with the confectioner's sugar.

Don Bowersox's Pumpkin Bread

MY FATHER DON IS FAMOUS in our family for his moist, perfectly spiced Pumpkin Bread. It's so delicious and versatile that it can be served for breakfast, toasted and spread with sweet butter, or enjoyed as an afternoon snack with a mug of hot apple cider following a skating or caroling party. Best of all, it freezes beautifully which makes it ideal to have on hand for last-minute gift giving.

1½	cups sugar
½	cup cooking oil
2	eggs
1	16-ounce can pumpkin without spices
1¾	cups flour
¼	teaspoon baking powder
1	teaspoon salt
1	teaspoon baking soda
½	teaspoon ground cloves
½	teaspoon ground cinnamon
½	teaspoon ground nutmeg or freshly grated
½	teaspoon allspice
⅓	cup water
	Handful each raisins and nuts (optional)

Preheat the oven to 350°F. Grease 1 large or 2 small loaf pans.

In a large mixing bowl, combine the sugar and oil. Add the remaining ingredients and mix well. Pour into the prepared loaf pan and bake for 1 hour. Cool on wire racks.

Banana Nut Bread

Every family has their own favorite recipe for this delicately flavored bread. This version, tested by many members of the Bowersox clan, wins raves every time it's served. It's a terrific way to use up over-ripe bananas, and it freezes well, so having some loaves stashed in the freezer for last-minute gifts is easy. Try slices toasted and spread with whipped cream cheese or a fruit preserve for a light breakfast.

½ cup sugar

⅓ cup unsalted butter

2 eggs

1¾ cups flour

1 teaspoon baking powder

½ teaspoon baking soda

½ teaspoon salt

1 cup mashed ripe bananas

½ cup chopped walnuts

Preheat the oven to 350°F. Butter and flour a 9 x 5 x 3-inch loaf pan.

Using an electric mixer, beat the sugar and butter for 1 minute. Stop and scrape down the sides and beat for another minute. Reduce the speed and add the eggs. Beat for 30 seconds. Stop and scrape the bowl. Return to high speed and beat for 1½ minutes.

Sift together the dry ingredients. Working at a low speed, add half the dry ingredients and half of the mashed bananas. Mix for 30 seconds and add the remaining dry ingredients and bananas. Mix for an additional 30 seconds. Stop and scrape the bowl. Blend in the walnuts and combine well.

Pour the mixture into the prepared pan and bake for 40 to 45 minutes. Remove from the pan and cool on a wire rack.

Brandied Apricot Jam

MAKES 3 8-OUNCE JARS

APRICOTS AND ALMONDS ARE one of the most delightful pairings of flavors in the kitchen, especially in a conserve. The subtle accents of nutmeg and brandy make this jam even more enticing, while its sweet fruit flavor makes it a natural companion to pork and poultry, as well as toasted English muffins and crumpets.

Be sure to use dried apricots with the pits already removed.

1	orange
2	cups halved dried apricots
2½	cups water
1¼	cups sugar
½	teaspoon almond extract
¼	teaspoon freshly grated nutmeg or ground
3	tablespoons brandy

Remove the zest from the orange and squeeze its juice into a small, heavy saucepot. Add to the pot the apricots, orange zest and water. Cover and refrigerate overnight.

The next day, bring the mixture to a boil, lower the heat and simmer for 5 minutes. Add the sugar and continue to boil, stirring gently and continuously for about 20 minutes. When the mixture becomes thick, be careful not to crush the apricots. Remove from the heat, add the almond extract, nutmeg and brandy and mix gently.

Pour into sterilized jars and cover with the lids. Allow to mellow for a couple of weeks before serving. May be kept for several months.

Creole Jam

THIS FRUITY, BANANA-BASED *condiment is a delicious accompaniment to roasted turkey or baked ham. Ground cloves, freshly grated nutmeg and the surprise of lime juice—along with some hearty rum—give this jam its sophisticated, tropical flavor. Try it on your favorite bread or muffin. Use decorative canning jars or personalize them with colorful labels to make your gifts even more special.*

3 pounds bananas

2 pounds superfine sugar

1 ¼ cups water

3 limes

¼ teaspoon ground cloves

¼ teaspoon freshly grated nutmeg
or ground

⅔ cup rum

Peel and cut the bananas into 2-inch chunks. Blanch them in boiling water for 1 minute. Drain. Bring the sugar and water to a boil and add the bananas. Simmer for ½ hour.

Remove the zest from the limes and squeeze the juice into the banana syrup. Add the zest and the spices. Simmer for 20 minutes. Remove from the heat and add the rum. Mix well and pour into sterilized jars.

Cover with the lids and turn upside down until cooled.

Mint Jelly

THIS IS A TRUE MINT JELLY, delicate and not overpowering. Made with fresh mint leaves, which are now available with the fresh herbs in the produce section of most markets, it needs just a few drops of green food coloring to enhance its appearance. Served as a traditional condiment with a Christmas rack of lamb, the subtle mint flavor of this delicious homemade jelly will be a welcome surprise.

2 cups fresh mint leaves

2 cups water

⅓ cup lemon juice

Pinch of salt

3½ cups sugar

6 ounces liquid pectin

2 drops green food coloring

Lightly chop the mint and place it in a large saucepot. Add the water and bring to a boil. Remove from the heat, cover and allow it to steep for 15 minutes.

Pour the tea through a fine sieve into another large saucepot. Press on the mint to extract its entire flavor. Add the lemon juice, salt and sugar.

Bring the mixture to a rolling boil for 3 minutes. Add the pectin and return to a boil for another 3 minutes. Remove from the heat.

Skim off any foam from the surface and stir in the food coloring. Pour into hot, sterilized jars and seal with the lids. Cool and store indefinitely.

Pear Chutney

CHUTNEYS FOUND THEIR WAY TO Western dining tables thanks to the English who encountered them during their colonial days in India and wholeheartedly adopted the spicy, sweet and sour condiment. British chutneys, however, differ from the Indian staple by having the consistency of jam and being primarily sweet and spicy. Try a medley of ripe pears for this autumn version. Bosc, Bartlett and Comice all have delicious flavors and will stand up well to the spices.

- 2 large onions, finely diced
- ¼ cup vegetable oil
- 8 ripe pears, peeled, diced into ½-inch dice
- 1 medium red bell pepper, finely diced
- 6 tablespoons brown sugar
- ¼ cup sugar
- 1 cup molasses
- ¼ cup raisins
- ½ cup orange juice
- 1 teaspoon salt
- ½ teaspoon freshly ground pepper
- ½ teaspoon ground coriander
- ½ cup white vinegar
- 2 tablespoons lemon juice
- 2 teaspoons chopped fresh mint

In a large, heavy sauté pan over high heat, cook the onion in the vegetable oil. Add the pears and cook for 2 to 3 minutes more. Add the remaining ingredients except the vinegar, lemon juice and mint. Bring to a simmer and cook over low heat for 1 hour, stirring occasionally. Add a small amount of orange juice if the sauce seems to be drying out.

Remove from the heat and add the vinegar, lemon juice and mint. Mix well. Remove to 8-ounce jars, allow to cool. Can be kept in refrigerator for about 3 weeks.

Cranberry Ketchup

MAKES 6 8-OUNCE JARS

WHO SAID KETCHUP COULD be made only from tomatoes? Cranberries and red wine vinegar give this fruity version its rich garnet color, while golden raisins, fresh orange juice and dark brown sugar provide the sweetness. Blended smooth in a food processor, this flavorful condiment will lend its delicious taste to everything from hamburgers to meat loaf and homemade French fries—and make a truly unique Christmas gift.

4	tomatoes
12	ounces cranberries
1	medium onion, diced
1½	cups red wine vinegar
1	cup dark brown sugar
½	cup golden raisins
2	teaspoons onion powder
1	teaspoon orange zest
½	teaspoon freshly ground pepper
¼	teaspoon ground cumin
½	teaspoon salt
	Juice of 1 orange

In a medium saucepot, bring all of the ingredients to a boil. Lower the heat until the mixture simmers and cook for 45 minutes. Stir occasionally. Remove from the heat and allow to cool.

Place the mixture in the bowl of a food processor. Pulse until it is blended, but still chunky. Pour into sterilized jars, cover and refrigerate for up to 2 weeks.

Cranberry Chutney

MAKES 4 8-OUNCE JARS

PLUMP RED CRANBERRIES SIMMERED in a spicy sauce with pear, apple and onion chunks create a sweet and spicy chutney that will tantalize everyone's taste buds and enhance meat or poultry main dishes. Use fresh or frozen berries for the best flavor. For another taste sensation, try this condiment as a low-fat alternative to butter on baked potatoes and rice.

12	ounces cranberries
1	large apple, diced
1	pear, diced
1	large onion, diced
2	green onions, chopped
10	garlic cloves, minced
2	tablespoons freshly grated gingerroot
1	teaspoon ground coriander
½	teaspoon ground cumin
¾	cup dark brown sugar
½	cup golden raisins
2¼	cups red wine vinegar

In a large saucepot, combine all of the ingredients and bring to a boil. Simmer over medium heat, stirring occasionally, for ½ hour. Remove from the heat.

When the mixture is cool, pour into sterilized jars and refrigerate for up to 1 month.

Gifts from the Kitchen

Tangerine-Fig Relish

MAKES 4 8-OUNCE JARS

FOR ME, DISCOVERING TANGERINES in the market is one of the first signs of the Christmas season. Just seeing their burst of orange brightens dark December days. To enjoy their zesty citrus flavor later in the winter, pair tangerines with dried figs in this novel sweet and sour relish that's a first cousin to chutney. Choose a good-quality vinegar of at least five percent acid content to ensure the proper tartness.

1 pound dried figs, chopped
1 red onion, diced
½ cup orange juice
¾ cup cider vinegar
¼ cup brown sugar
1 tablespoon tangerine zest
2 tangerines, peeled, sectioned, seeded

In a large, heavy saucepot, combine all of the ingredients. Bring to a boil, lower the heat and simmer, stirring occasionally, for ½ hour. Pour into sterilized canning jars. Seal with the lids and turn upside down until cool.

Chestnut Pieces in Syrup

MAKES 3 8-OUNCE JARS

ALTHOUGH THE NAME "CHESTNUT" has been given to many nuts, it refers primarily to nuts from the European "sweet" or "Spanish" chestnut tree, as well as to its American and Asian botanical cousins. Spooning some of these Chestnut Pieces in Syrup over vanilla ice cream makes a quick and easy dessert, which is elegant enough to serve at a dinner party. In fact, the classic coupe aux marrons *with ice cream was the predecessor to what we now know as an ice cream sundae.*

½ pound dried chestnuts

3 cups water

1 cup sugar

½ cup light corn syrup

1 teaspoon vanilla extract

3 tablespoons brandy

Cover the chestnuts in water and refrigerate overnight. Over medium heat, bring them to a simmer and cook for 1 to 3 hours, until they are soft. Drain and cool. Cut the chestnuts into ½-inch pieces.

In a medium saucepot, bring the water, sugar and corn syrup to a boil. Add the chestnuts and simmer until the syrup is reduced by half. Remove from the heat and add the vanilla extract and brandy. Stir well and pour into sterilized jars. Cover and refrigerate for up to 4 months.

Chocolate Sauce

THE VARIATIONS POSSIBLE WITH this basic chocolate dessert sauce make it the ideal holiday gift because it can be easily adapted for everyone on your list. Coffee lovers will enjoy indulging with Mocha Sauce, candy cane fans will appreciate the Chocolate-Peppermint Sauce, and Caribbean vacationers will enjoy the tropical flavors of Chocolate-Orange Sauce. The hardest part will be saving a jar for yourself.

2 cups water

2 cups sugar

1 cup light corn syrup

2½ cups unsweetened cocoa

2 teaspoons vanilla extract

2 tablespoons unsalted butter

In a small, heavy saucepot over high heat, bring the water, sugar and corn syrup to a boil. Lower the heat, cover and simmer for 2 minutes. Remove from the heat.

Sift in the cocoa, add the vanilla extract and butter and mix well. Pour into sterilized jars, cover and refrigerate for up to a month.

Variations

MOCHA SAUCE: Add 2 tablespoons of powdered, instant espresso to the water or replace 1 cup of the water with 1 cup of very strong coffee.

CREAMY CHOCOLATE SAUCE: Replace 1 cup of the water with 1 cup of light cream.

CHOCOLATE-ORANGE SAUCE: Replace the vanilla extract with 2 tablespoons of Grand Marnier.

CHOCOLATE-PEPPERMINT SAUCE: Replace the vanilla extract with ½ teaspoon of peppermint extract.

Butterscotch Sauce

A ONE-TIME INVESTMENT in a candy thermometer opens up an entire world of desserts. This sauce is simple to make and unusually delicate in flavor. It is well worth having the equipment on hand so that this recipe can be made often for your own home as well as for gift giving.

1½ cups light brown sugar

1 cup maple syrup

⅓ cup unsalted butter

½ teaspoon salt

¼ cup water

2 teaspoons vanilla extract

1 cup heavy cream

In a heavy, medium-size saucepot, stirring constantly, heat the brown sugar, maple syrup, butter, salt and water to a boil. Stop stirring and lower the heat so that it stays at a boil without overflowing the pot, until a candy thermometer reads 235°F. Remove from the heat, let cool for 10 minutes, and then mix in the vanilla extract and cream until smooth.

Pour into sterilized jars. Cover and refrigerate for up to a month.

Index

127